TOP 10

P9-CKO-746

TURKEY'S
SOUTHWEST COAST

MATT WILLIS

EYEWITNESS TRAVEL

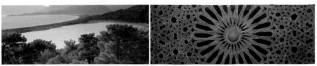

Left **İztuzu Beach and freshwater lagoon** Right **Detail of ceiling, Eşrefoğlu Mosque, Beyşehir**

LONDON, NEW YORK,
MELBOURNE, MUNICH AND DELHI
www.dk.com

Produced by Coppermill Books
55 Salop Road, London E17 7HS
Reproduced by Colourscan, Singapore
Printed and bound in China by
Leo Paper Products Ltd

First American Edition, 2012

12 13 14 15 10 9 8 7 6 5 4 3 2 1

Published in the United States by
DK Publishing, 375 Hudson Street,
New York, New York 10014

Published in Great Britain by Dorling Kindersley Ltd

A catalog record for this book is
available from the Library of Congress.

ISSN 1479-344X
ISBN 978 0 7566 7073 3

Within each Top 10 list in this book, no hierarchy of
quality or popularity is implied. All 10 are, in the
editor's opinion, of roughly equal merit.

MIX
Paper from
responsible sources
FSC™ C018179
www.fsc.org

Contents

Top 10 of Turkey's Southwest Coast

Left **Ruined theatre at Hierapolis** Right **The beach at Adrasan**

Left **Temple of Athena, Priene, near Kuşadası** Right **İçmeler Beach, Marmaris**

Key to abbreviations Adm *admission charge* Free *no admission charge*

TOP 10 OF TURKEY'S SOUTHWEST COAST

🔟 Turkey's Southwest Coast Highlights

With fascinating ruins, top-class tourist facilities and superb weather virtually guaranteed, this glorious stretch of coastline has something for everyone. Resorts ranging from compact and exclusive to large and bustling offer all-inclusive packages, while independent visitors can opt for comfortable hotels or self-catering accommodation in tranquil seaside locations. The broad variety of activities and excursions available in high season means there needn't be a dull moment.

Antalya 1

The main point of arrival for most visitors to the coast, Antalya is a busy modern city with an ancient heart. Close to several major sites, it's an ideal base for day trips *(see pp8–11)*.

Termessos 2
This remarkable hilltop site is partially overgrown and often lost in the clouds. Once a powerful and independent city protected by great stone walls, Termessos' monumental ruins include a stunningly situated theatre and some striking rock tombs *(see pp12–13)*.

Ephesus 3
As the ancient capital of the Roman province of Asia, Ephesus was a grand city second only to Rome. Many splendid buildings have been unearthed; some, like the Celsus Library, have been restored to their former glory *(see pp14–17)*.

Pamukkale and Hierapolis 4
Pamukkale's glistening white travertine pools have drawn visitors since Roman times when the spa town of Hierapolis grew up around them *(see pp18–19)*.

The Lycian Way 5

Tracking the coastline for over 500 km (313 miles), this well-marked hiking trail takes in unspoiled villages, mountain ranges, desolate ruins and isolated bays *(see pp20–21)*.

Preceding pages **Lycian tombs at Myra (see p83)**

Alanya 7
Set beside a rocky promontory that rises majestically from the sea, the attractions offered by this hugely popular resort include a wild nightlife, sandy beaches and the rock's medieval ruins *(see pp24–25)*.

Side 6
Before the Romans, Side was home to pirates and slave-traders. These days it's a bustling tourist centre where shops, restaurants and *pensions* are intermingled with the ruins *(see pp22–23)*.

Marmaris 8
With some of the coast's best night-life, a superb marina, myriad shopping opportunities and a seafront jammed with mile after mile of lively bars and restaurants, Marmaris is a perennial favourite for package tourists from all over Europe and beyond *(see pp26–27)*.

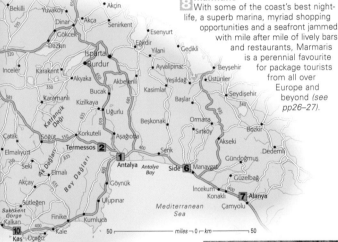

Kaş 10
This small coastal town with a relaxed ambience, laid-back cafés and quirky craft shops has retained a distinct Turkish flavour despite its high population of foreign tourists *(see pp30–31)*.

Fethiye 9
Particularly popular with British tourists, Fethiye is a pleasant seaside town surrounded by wooded hills. Ancient highlights include majestic Lycian tombs and a theatre facing the harbour *(see pp28–29)*.

Antalya

Established as a naval base for King Attalus II in the 2nd century BC, Antalya evolved under alternating periods of Christian and Muslim domination that ended with its absorption into the Ottoman Empire in the 15th century. Today, vast hotels and apartment blocks line the city's superb beaches at Konyaaltı and Lara, and the region's farmland and greenhouses provide over 60 per cent of Turkey's fruit and vegetable needs. The enormously atmospheric Old Town (Kaleiçi) remains the focus for visitors to this vibrant city.

Hadrian's Gate

⊘ If you are staying in Kaleiçi and have a car, take a ticket at the barrier and make sure that the hotel registers your vehicle so that you can drive in and out of the area without charge.

⊜ When visiting one of Antalya's high-end nightclubs, check the menu before ordering; drinks prices are often four or five times what they are in less exclusive establishments.

• Map H5 • Antalya Tourist Information Centre: Selçuk Mah, Mermerli Sok, Kaleiçi; (0242) 247 05 41; www. antalyakulturturizm.gov.tr
• Archaeological Museum: Kenan Evren Bulvari, Konyaaltı; (0242) 238 56 88; Open 9am–5pm Tue–Sun; Adm; www. antalyamuzesi.gov.tr

Top 10 Features

1. Konyaaltı Beach
2. Archaeological Museum
3. Yivli Minaret
4. Clock Tower (Saat Kulesi)
5. Old Town (Kaleiçi)
6. Tekeli Mehmet Paşa Mosque
7. Hadrian's Gate
8. Korkut Minaret
9. Hıdırlık Tower
10. Karaalioğlu Park

Archaeological Museum

Packed with sarcophagi *(above)*, mosaics and other relics from nearby sites, this museum – one of Turkey's best – offers a fascinating insight into the region's past.

Yivli Minaret

Built on the orders of Sultan Alaeddin Keykubad in the 13th century, this elegant fluted minaret can be seen from all around the Old Town.

Clock Tower (Saat Kulesi)

One of a pair of towers that once guarded the main entrance of the Old Town, the Clock Tower *(right)* takes its name from a 19th-century addition to the original structure.

Konyaaltı Beach

Antalya's famous pebble beach *(main image)*, awarded a Blue Flag for cleanliness, is a picturesque sight as it arcs towards the distant Toros mountains.

For more on the Archaeological Museum See pp10–11.

Old Town (Kaleiçi)
With its maze of narrow cobbled streets, old Ottoman houses, secluded gardens, plentiful tea houses and ancient Roman walls, Kaleiçi *(above)* is a delight to explore.

Tekeli Mehmet Paşa Mosque
This single-domed mosque *(right)* dates back to the end of the 16th century. The interior is unadorned, and punctuated with simple coloured glass windows.

Hadrian's Gate
Though it now stands well below street level, this magnificent triple-arched gate was once one of the city's main entrances. It was built to honour a visit by Emperor Hadrian in AD 130.

King Attalus II
Intent on maintaining control of his expanding kingdom, Attalus II (220–138 BC), king of Pergamon and an accomplished military leader, founded Attalia (Antalya) to serve as a base for his powerful navy. According to legend, the site was chosen after he ordered his men to find him "paradise on earth" – which it certainly must have seemed at the time, with its forested hills, idyllic golden beaches and stunning mountain backdrop.

Hıdırlık Tower
Built from honey-coloured stone and showing few signs of decay, this squat cylindrical tower has stood here since the second century AD.

Korkut Minaret
Part of a mosque built by Şehzade Korkut in the 15th century, this unusual minaret lost its upper half during a fire in 1846.

Karaalioğlu Park
This delightful, well-tended park *(right)* runs parallel with the cliffs to the east of town. Dotted with statues and pretty flower-beds, it's a lovely place to escape from the heat.

For more on the Korkut (also known as the Kesik Minare, or "cut minaret") mosque See p49.

Left **Gallery of the Gods** Centre **Detail of Dionysos Sarcophagus** Right **Display of coins**

🔟 Antalya Archaeological Museum

1 Gallery of the Gods
The statues in this gallery were discovered in Aspendos *(see p97)* and Perge *(see p89)*. They date from the 2nd and 3rd centuries AD and once adorned temples and fine buildings. Most common are those of Apollo, the sun god, and Artemis, the goddess of hunting. Hygieia, the goddess of health (the origin of the word "hygiene"), is depicted with a snake, a symbol long associated with medicine.

2 Perge Statue Gallery
Painstakingly reassembled by archaeologists, these larger-than-life statues were found in pieces beneath Perge's theatre, which collapsed during an earth-quake. Depicting both gods and emperors, perhaps the most imposing are those of Hadrian, Trajan and Alexander the Great.

3 Mosaic Hall
Several large mosaics uncovered at Seleukia *(see p98)* are on display here. Among them is the Philosopher's Mosaic, which features portraits of celebrated intellectuals such as Pythagoras, Herodotos and Salon. Though little of the original piece remains, the detail and colouring of the two surviving faces is remarkable.

4 Stone-Age Tools
Arranged chronologically, the museum's exhibits begin with a large display of finds from the Paleolithic Era, when a number of caves in the region were inhabited by primitive humans. Many of the artifacts – including stone blades, axe heads and simple figures – were discovered at Karain Cave *(see p90)*.

5 Sarcophagi Hall
From child-sized to gigantic, this stunning array of intricately carved sarcophagi originated in the vast necropolises of ancient Perge. Many were smuggled to Europe and the USA in the last century and have subsequently been returned to form part of the museum's collection.

6 Bronze-Age Burial Urns
During the early Bronze Age (3000–2000 BC) it was the custom to arrange the dead inside clay urns buried horizontally in the ground – as in the large necropolises that have been unearthed close to Elmalı *(see p82)*. Several examples of such urns are exhibited here. The skeletons lie huddled in the foetal position, surrounded by their weapons and jewellery.

Bronze-age burial urn with skeleton

7 Hall of Coins

Hundreds of glinting coins fill rows of display cases on the museum's first floor, the earliest dating back to the 7th century BC. Also on display are large hauls of silver and gold coins found at Side and Aspendos.

Anatolian costume in the Ethnographic Hall

9 Ethnographic Hall

Noted for their intricate embroidery and vivid colours, Anatolian dresses like the ones exhibited here were worn on a daily basis until the 20th century. Men's garments include şalvar – baggy white trousers still worn in rural areas.

8 Bones of St Nicholas

Occupying a small shrine in a corner of the museum's first floor are what are purported to be holy relics of St Nicholas, whose kind deeds gave rise to the legend of Santa Claus. They include a jawbone with a tooth, and several bones in a velvet-covered chest.

10 Antique Carpets

The final hall is dedicated to a display of carpets, several dating from the 16th century. Some show signs of wear and tear, but all are incredibly well-made, with designs that link them to the school of carpet-weaving in nearby Doşemealti.

Top 10 Gods

1. Zeus/Jupiter – king of the gods, with power over natural forces
2. Apollo – god of sunlight, poetry and the fine arts
3. Aphrodite/Venus – goddess of love and beauty
4. Athena/Minerva – goddess of war, wisdom and science
5. Artemis/Diana – goddess of hunting and nature
6. Nemesis – goddess of heavenly revenge
7. Hermes/Mercury – messenger of the gods
8. Hera/Juno – chief goddess, through her marriage to Zeus
9. Asclepios/Vediovis – god of physicians and father of Hygieia
10. Hygieia – goddess of health

Worshipping the Gods

The Greeks and Romans started out as cult worshippers. The benevolence of their gods was maintained not by good behaviour, but by strict ritual observance. In Greek and Roman homes, it was even common to "invite" gods to dinner, setting a place for them at the table and serving food to ensure their favours. The spread of Christianity in the first and second centuries AD is partly attributed to St Paul's missions in Anatolia. At that time, there were frequent conflicts with the dominant pagans, which led to sporadic periods of persecution of Christians until 313 AD, when Emperor Constantine declared freedom for all religions. Christianity was officially adopted as the Empire's religion towards the end of the 4th century.

Hermes, messenger of the gods

TOP 10 Termessos

Perched high on a mountain plateau, the ancient city of Termessos entered the history books in 333 BC, when Alexander the Great decided not to risk attacking what he described as "an eagle's nest". Its very inaccessibility has kept much of the city from being excavated, and the parts that have been examined are rapidly disappearing again under dense undergrowth. Nonetheless, the site's sheer size and the monumental structures that remain – mostly dating back to the Roman period – make for an immensely rewarding visit.

Detail of sarcophagus in the southwest necropolis

🌀 Carry bottled water and sun protection, and allow at least two hours to explore the ruins.

🔵 The only source of refreshments is the small restaurant just past the entry barrier.

- Map H4
- (0242) 23 85 688
- Open 9am–7pm
- Adm
- www.antalyamuzesi.gov.tr

Top 10 Features

1. Theatre
2. City Walls
3. Necropolises
4. Tombs
5. Tomb of Alcetas
6. Cisterns
7. Güllük Daği Milli Park
8. Spectacular Views
9. Bouleuterion
10. Gymnasium and Baths

City Walls

The city was protected by a network of massive upper and lower walls. The remains of the lower section are just visible as you approach Termessos, while the upper walls *(below)* rise majestically from the undergrowth at the city's entrance.

Tombs

Several impressive tombs have been cut into the cliffs to the west of the site. Large sarcophagi stand on flat rocks in the vicinity; many more lie deep in the undergrowth or high in the cliffs above.

Theatre

Set high on a clifftop and often lost in the clouds, the theatre *(main image)* couldn't be more dramatically located. Built during the Hellenistic era, it had seating for 4,200.

Necropolises

There are necropolises to the northeast and southwest *(below)*, outside the city walls. The northeastern necropolis, (by the car park) is easiest to access. It's possible to discern the outlines of individual tombs in the scattered ruins.

Termessos is thought to have been abandoned when an earthquake destroyed the aqueduct providing its water supply.

Tomb of Alcetas
5 Alcetas was a heroic general from Pisidia who took refuge in Termessos but was betrayed by the city's elders. Rather than allow them to hand him over to his enemy, Alcetas killed himself. The tomb *(detail above)* was cut into the cliff by his followers.

Cisterns
6 Cavernous cisterns stored vital water supplies for the arid settlement. Most of them have collapsed or are inaccessible, but the ones that have survived near the agora give an impression of their awesome capacity.

Güllük Daği Milli Park
7 Termessos lies within Güllük Daği Milli Park (also called Termessos National Park), after Güllük Daği, the mountain that dominates the landscape *(below)*. There are around 113 bird and 680 plant species here, as well as wolves, jackals and deer.

Gymnasium and Baths
10 The size and central location of this huge building, now reduced to its southern façade *(above)*, show how important such facilities were to the locals.

Spectacular Views
8 Termessos' hilltop location affords it an inexhaustible supply of great views. The best are from the upper city walls and from the theatre, which stands on a cliff-edge above two valleys.

Bouleuterion
9 One of Termessos' best-preserved structures, this vast building – which still stands over 10 m (33 ft) high – is thought to have been used for meetings or theatre performances in winter.

Alexander the Great

Born in Macedonia and educated by Aristotle, Alexander the Great (356–323 BC) began his legendary conquest of the Persian Empire in 334 BC. He reached Termessos a year later, and although he left the Lycian city untouched, countless other settlements either fell or opened their gates to him. His troops never lost a battle, and within nine years he had conquered the Persians and become ruler of a far-flung empire that stretched all the way from Greece to India.

Ephesus

Once the capital of the Roman province of Asia and second only to Rome in size and importance, Ephesus is Turkey's best-known archaeological site. Spread over a large area, the ruins – and particularly the Terrace Houses, which have been thoroughly excavated – provide a fascinating insight into life in an ancient Roman city. The great amphitheatre is as grand as ever, and the stunning Celsus Library, painstakingly reconstructed by archaeologists and engineers, is one of the country's most impressive ancient structures.

Gate of Augustus

🖝 Note that a map of this large site is not included with ticket purchases. To explore Ephesus independently, it's advisable to rent an audio guide or buy a map from one of the stalls outside the gates.

🅠 Although there are stalls selling snacks near the main gate, Selçuk's restaurants are the best option for a decent meal.

• Map A2
• (0232) 892 60 10
• Open 8am–6:30pm daily
• Adm
• Ephesus Museum: Atatürk Mah, Uğur Mumcu Sevgi Yolu, Selçuk; Map B2; (0232) 892 60 10; Open 8am–7pm daily (to 5pm in winter); Adm; www.selcuk.bel.tr

Top 10 Features

1. Celsus Library
2. Terrace Houses
3. Gate of Augustus
4. Theatre
5. Temple of Hadrian
6. Marble Street
7. Arcadian Way
8. Brothel
9. Cave of the Seven Sleepers
10. Ephesus Museum

Terrace Houses
Also known as the Houses on the Slope, these exclusive, mostly three-storey dwellings with running water *(below)* were home to the city's elite. Their murals and mosaic floors are remarkably well preserved. An extra entry fee applies.

Theatre
Founded during the Hellenistic period, the great theatre *(right)* underwent many alterations over the years. By the 2nd century AD, it had an elaborate three-tier stage building and an audience capacity of 25,000.

Celsus Library
Ephesus' most famous ruin, the Celsus Library *(main image)* was erected as a memorial to the governor of Rome's Asian province, Julius Celsus Polemaeanus (AD 92–114).

Gate of Augustus
Dedicated to the Emperor Augustus (27 BC–AD 14) by two of his freed slaves, this imposing triple-arched gate stands between the Celsus Library and the agora.

The Celsus Library's façade collapsed after an earthquake in the 10th century and was not reconstructed until the 1970s.

5 Temple of Hadrian
Worshippers would have entered the temple porch through the monumental arch that still stands *(above)*. Outside are four plinths – now empty – that bore statues of Roman emperors. An image of Tyche, the city's tutelary deity, guards the main entrance.

6 Marble Street
Also known as the Sacred Way, this street paved with great marble slabs *(right)* crosses the Arcadian Way and connects the theatre with the Celsus Library. The columns whose remnants run along either side would once have supported grand porticos.

7 Arcadian Way
Known as Harbour Street before it was renovated by Emperor Arcadius (AD 395–408), this grand parade ran between the harbour and the theatre. Flanked with porticos and mighty columns, it was lit up at night with 50 lamps.

The Lost Temple of Artemis

The Temple of Artemis at Ephesus was listed as one of the Seven Wonders of the Ancient World by the Greek poet Antipater of Sidon in the 1st century AD. A splendid construction built around 550 BC, it was destroyed and reconstructed a number of times before finally being dismantled in the 4th century AD. Today, just one of its original 127 columns marks the location of the temple's scattered foundations. A scale model of the temple is on display at Ephesus Museum.

8 Brothel
A street sign showing a foot next to a woman's head, and a clay statue with an enormous phallus mark out this modest building as a brothel.

10 Ephesus Museum
Occupying several halls and a courtyard, the museum *(above)* at nearby Selçuk contains a broad range of artifacts discovered at Ephesus, including two magnificent statues of Artemis.

9 Cave of the Seven Sleepers
Seven Christians sealed in this cave by Emperor Decius (AD 201–251) were allegedly found fast asleep when it was unsealed two centuries later.

For more on Ephesus Museum **See pp16–17.**

Left **Sarcophagus with muses** Right **Temple of Hadrian frieze, detail**

🔟 Ephesus Museum

1 Statues of Artemis
These two superb marble statues of the goddess Artemis date from the 1st and 2nd centuries AD; the earlier of the two is known as "Beautiful Artemis", the later as "Great Artemis". Both are adorned with images of sacred animals and rows of bulls' testicles, symbolizing fertility.

2 Emperor Cult Relics
Domitian (81–96 AD) was the first emperor to be honoured with a temple in Ephesus; the head and arms of his colossal 7-m- (23-ft-) high statue are on display alongside busts of various other emperors.

Statue of Artemis ("Beautiful Artemis")

3 Ephesus Monument
This 152-line carved stone inscription outlines the Emperor Nero's customs regulations from 62 AD, and includes details such as a "head tax" for traded slaves.

4 Eros Room
An entire gallery of the museum is given over to finds related to Eros, the god of love. They include clay lamps with his image, figurines and a bronze sculpture of Eros riding a dolphin.

5 Medical Instruments
Medicinal practice was well advanced in Ephesus. This fascinating display of glass vials, miniature tweezers, needles and a variety of other instruments is accompanied by texts describing routine operations during Roman times.

6 Sarcophagus with Muses
Exhibited in the courtyard, this large tomb contained the body of a wealthy female, whose image is carved onto the central niche of its side panel. She is flanked by the muses Euterpe, Clio, Calliope and Erato.

7 Roman House Room
This large gallery is taken up with finds from the Terrace Houses (see p14), including a recreation of the Socrates Room, famous for its 3rd-century mural depicting the renowned philosopher. Other exhibits include a magnificent 2nd-century bronze statue of Eros riding a dolphin, which once formed part of a fountain, and an intriguing folding stool made of iron.

In ancient times, worshippers would have dressed the statues of Artemis in expensive robes.

8 Temple of Hadrian Frieze

The first three panels of this four-panel frieze show the mythological foundation of Ephesus, including a depiction of Androclus hunting a wild boar. The fourth panel was added in the 4th century AD, after the rebuilding of the temple following a major earthquake in the region; it depicts the Emperor Theodosius with his family, surrounded by a group of gods. A copy of the frieze is installed in the remains of the temple in Ephesus.

Head of Zeus

9 Head of Zeus

This bust of Zeus was broken into two parts, which were found at separate locations and later matched. It once adorned a public fountain constructed during the 1st century AD.

10 Tomb Objects

During pre-Christian times it was common practice to place gifts in the tombs of the dead. The museum has a display of colourful glass vessels found in sarcophagi from different eras.

Top 10 Gladiators' Weapons

1 *Gladius* – long, narrow sword
2 *Iaculum* – weighted throwing-net
3 *Lancea* – short javelin
4 *Plumbatae* – lead-weighted darts
5 *Sphendone* – sling
6 *Spatha* – broadsword
7 *Pugnum* – small shield
8 *Pugio* – small dagger made of iron or bronze
9 *Fascina* – three-pronged metal trident
10 *Quadrens* – a dagger with four needle-like prongs at each corner of a square guard

Pugnum and *pugio*

Gladiators at Ephesus

Gladiator contests first became popular in the Roman Empire during the 1st century BC, and are thought to have reached Ephesus around 69 BC. To facilitate this bloodthirsty sport, Ephesus' Hellenistic stadium was converted into an oval arena that could hold 25,000 spectators. Intended to entertain and impress the public, gladiators fought until one or the other was overcome; a verdict of death or pardon was left up to the crowds, who supported their favourite gladiators rather like people support celebrity footballers today. The gladiators' graveyard uncovered at Ephesus in 1993 was the first discovery of its kind, and revealed that while the combatants received hideous injuries, they were provided with excellent medical treatment, indicative of their high value. The best were bought and sold for large sums. Bone analysis has also revealed that contrary to popular belief, gladiators were fat. They were fed a high-carb diet that developed fatty layers to protect their muscle from superficial wounds. The sport continued until the 4th century AD, when it was outlawed by Emperor Constantine.

A gladiator carved in stone in the ruins of Ephesus

Finds from Ephesus are also on display at the Ephesus Museum in Vienna and the British Museum in London.

Pamukkale and Hierapolis

Pamukkale means "cotton castle" in Turkish, but at first sight this remarkable natural phenomenon seems more like a frosty Arctic landscape. Pamukkale's travertines are actually brittle formations created by the calcium content of its thermal spring waters. The site of a temple as early as the 3rd century BC, it was developed as a spa town – Hierapolis – by Attalos, King of Pergamon (220–138 BC), and later ceded to the bath-loving Romans, who built most of the structures to be seen today. The best time to visit is evening or early morning.

Remains of Basilica built over Roman bathhouse

Both Pamukkale and Hierapolis are open for 24 hours a day throughout the year. A single ticket covers entry to the whole site, excluding museum entry and swimming in the Antique Pool. A free bus shuttles visitors from Hierapolis' upper entrance to the Antique Pool and back every 15 minutes between 8am and 7pm.

The café at the Antique Pool serves food, but tends to get overwhelmed by large groups during the day. The quieter kiosks at the upper entrance have simple snacks and drinks.

- Map E2
- (0258) 272 20 44
- Open 8am–7pm
- Adm
- www.pamukkale.org.tr
- Archaeological Museum: Open 9am–7pm Tue–Sun; Adm

Top 10 Features

1. Travertine Terraces
2. Antique Pool
3. Necropolis
4. Theatre
5. Basilica
6. Arch of Domitian
7. Colonnaded Street
8. Southern Bath
9. St Philip Martyrium
10. Archaeological Museum

Travertine Terraces

The sight of an entire hillside of dazzling white terraces overflowing with aquamarine waters *(main image)* has entranced visitors for millennia. The addition of artificial travertines has detracted little from the overall spectacle.

Antique Pool

During Roman times, Pamukkale's main spring was used as a bath. Now that it supplies an outdoor pool littered with ancient columns *(above)*, the private owners have transformed the antique bathing experience into a highly profitable industry.

Necropolis

With its profusion of house tombs, the necropolis feels more like a suburb than a graveyard. A typical tomb *(below)* is on two levels; some of the more elaborate feature windows and courtyards.

Theatre
4 Richly decorated with statues and carved reliefs, this impressively located 2nd-century-AD theatre *(above)* had a capacity of 20,000.

Basilica
5 Hierapolis had several basilicas. The ruins of one of the largest, built in the 6th century AD over a bathhouse, are fronted by two tall arches leaning at precarious angles.

Colonnaded Street
7 Archaeologists have re-erected a few of the columns that once flanked this broad, marble-paved street *(right)* – apart from these evocative remnants, only the foundations of shops and houses are left.

Southern Bath
8 A short distance from the travertines, the largest of Hierapolis' baths now houses the Archaeological Museum. A major restoration project has given a new lease of life to its broad arches, vaulted ceilings and massive walls.

Arch of Domitian
6 This 14-m- (46-ft-) wide triple-arched entrance flanked by two circular towers stands at the northern end of the colonnaded street. It was built in the 1st century AD by the then proconsul of Asia Julius Frontinus, in honour of his emperor.

Saved by World Heritage Status

Unregulated tourist development during the 1980s – including the construction of hotels, and a road directly over the travertines – caused terrible damage to Pamukkale. It was saved when UNESCO declared it a World Heritage Site in 1987. As a result, the hotels were pulled down, pools were built over the road, and access to the travertines was restricted to the artificial pools on the upper levels. Nowadays, the flow of water is controlled to ensure that the site retains its brilliant whiteness.

St Philip Martyrium
9 On the hilltop north of the site lie the ruins of a martyrium built in the 5th century AD in memory of Saint Philip, one of the twelve apostles. He was crucified upside down at Hierapolis in AD 87.

Archaeological Museum
10 This absorbing collection fills several of the great vaulted halls that once formed the Southern Bath. Among the exhibits are some superb examples of exquisitely decorated sarcophagi and marble reliefs *(right)*.

🔟 The Lycian Way

Traversing ancient ruins, isolated villages, glorious beaches and cloud-covered mountains, the Lycian Way makes for an incredible experience, far removed from that of most visitors to the Turkish coast. Marked in 2000 by British hiker and long-term Turkish resident Kate Clow, the path meanders for 509 km (318 miles) around the coast of ancient Lycia. The whole route takes four or five weeks to complete, but walkers can pick and choose shorter stretches from its various sections; the westernmost, from Fethiye to Patara, is particularly popular – and relatively easy. Parts of the trail are physically challenging, but adventures and unforgettable memories are guaranteed.

Views of Kaş

🕮 Hikers are strongly recommended to take with them Kate Clow's book *The Lycian Way* for a detailed description of the route.

💧 Top up your water supplies whenever you can as water points are far apart, and may be dry.

• Map E5–H5
• (0242) 243 11 48
• www.lycianway.com

Top 10 Features

1. Paragliders
2. Butterfly Valley
3. Patara Beach
4. Views of Kaş
5. Sunken Ruins
6. Ridge-Top Walk
7. Lighthouse
8. Adrasan
9. Mount Olympos
10. Göynük Canyon

Paragliders
As hikers follow the Lycian Way towards the village of Kirme, swarms of paragliders circle overhead *(main image)*, as they make their descent towards the beautiful beach at Ölüdeniz below.

Butterfly Valley
This lovely, butterfly-filled valley *(see p82)* can be accessed by sea, or by a precipitous inland path from the farming village of Faralya.

Patara Beach
A section of the Lycian Way brings hikers down from the hills to Patara, an ancient Lycian city with one of the south coast's best beaches *(right)*; it stretches for 12 unspoiled kilometres (7½ miles).

Views of Kaş
From the jumbled ruins of Phellos *(see p82)*, a steep path leads down to the sea. Hidden from sight by a lower ridge for much of the walk, a glorious view of Kaş and the scattered islands beyond is revealed partway through the descent.

➡️ *If you choose to paraglide, make sure that insurance is included with your flight – your general travel insurance is unlikely to cover you.*

Sunken Ruins
Following a sharp descent from Kılıçlı, an easy 15-km (9-mile) walk tracks the shoreline eastwards past the ruins of Aperlae to Üçağiz. A popular tourist destination, the village is a short boat or kayak trip away from the sunken ruins of Kekova *(above)*.

Ridge-Top Walk
This trek across a long, cedar-covered ridge *(below)* at an altitude of almost 1,800 m (5,905 ft) is the culmination of a difficult three-day walk from Zeytin to Finike. Visible far below, the sparkling sea is reached by a speedier descent.

Lighthouse
In a picturesque spot atop steep cliffs is the Gelidonya lighthouse. If the keeper is in when you arrive, he may let you climb to the top. The walk from Karaöz to Adrasan takes 6 to 7 hours.

Mount Olympos
Mount Olympos *(above)* (Tahtali Dağı in Turkish) reaches a height of 2,366 m (7,762 ft). The challenging ascent should only be attempted with the right preparations and equipment. The Olympos Teleferik cable car *(see p90)* offers a gentler way of reaching the summit.

Adrasan
Nestling in a sheltered bay with a clean pebble beach and transparent sea, this peaceful resort of small *pensions* and cafés offers a well-deserved rest after the tricky path from Gelidonya lighthouse.

Göynük Canyon
From the tiny village of Ovacik a path leads east into the forested Göynük valley, which narrows as it descends into a rocky canyon where walkers can slosh their way through shallow stream waters.

Local Hospitality
One of the most rewarding aspects of hiking along the Lycian Way is the experience of encountering the genuine curiosity and hospitality of villagers who are isolated from tourism, and likely to insist that you visit their homes for a glass of tea, dinner or even a bed for the night. The only language spoken will be Turkish, so a phrasebook will certainly help.

For more on the sunken ruins of Kekova **See p81.**

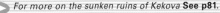

ᵀᴼᴾ10 Side

One of the busiest ports in the region during the Roman era, the peninsula town of Side was crammed with hundreds of small shops trading products and materials imported from all over Europe and North Africa. Today, unlike most ruined settlements, Side is once again a thriving commercial centre. The Roman colonnaded street – the high street of its day – is now Liman Caddesi, where visitors can browse in the Ottoman-styled shops that have sprung up to serve the tourist trade. There's even a nightclub built in the ruins of a temple beside the harbour.

Pottery on display at the Roman Baths Museum

🗗 If you are travelling by car, make sure that you park at the official car park just beyond the museum; otherwise you run the risk of having your vehicle towed.

🍷 Have a memorable evening drink at the Apollo Club (see p101), ensconced within Side's ruins.

• Map K5
• Side Tourist Information Centre: near the theatre; (0242) 753 12 65
• Side Roman Baths Museum: Selimiye Köyü; (0242) 753 10 06; Open 9am–7:30pm Tue–Sun; Adm

Top 10 Features

1. Monumental Gate
2. Temples of Apollo and Athena
3. Theatre
4. City Walls
5. Vespasian Monument
6. Roman Baths Museum
7. Byzantine Church
8. Side Village
9. Harbour
10. Beaches

2 Temples of Apollo and Athena

Of these two neighbouring temples, it is the partially reconstructed Temple of Apollo *(main image)* that has become Side's most photographed structure; its fine marble columns frame a superb view of the sea beyond.

3 Theatre

This 17,000-capacity theatre *(above)* was built in the 2nd century AD. When gladiatorial combat with wild animals became popular, a thick wall was built on the lower levels to protect spectators.

1 Monumental Gate

Little remains of the main city gate in the outer walls, but the 13-m- (43-ft-) high Monumental Gate, which gave access to the inner city in Roman times, has survived remarkably well.

4 City Walls

Side's original wall *(below)* was built in the 2nd century BC. An inner wall was built in the 4th century AD, to defend the city's shrunken boundaries.

5 Vespasian Monument

Mounted upon a double-stepped podium beside the Monumental Gate, this elegant but empty niche *(above)* bears a dedicatory inscription to the Emperor Vespasian (9–79 AD). The niche originally held a statue; later on, a fountain.

6 Roman Baths Museum

Side's largest Roman bathhouse was built in the 5th century AD. Now it houses the museum, where an absorbing collection of statues and sarcophagi are on display, alongside delicate pieces of jewellery and pottery.

7 Byzantine Church

In a colonnaded street within the original city walls are the remains of a large Byzantine Church built during the 5th century AD using stones and architectural fragments from Roman buildings.

8 Side Village

Quiet Side *(above)* is an odd mixture of shops, guest houses, restaurants and ruins. Few vehicles are permitted entry.

9 Harbour

The small harbour at the end of the peninsula was once a bustling port. Today, it's a calm spot providing moorage for yachts and small fishing boats, as well as boat trips to Manavgat Falls and Alanya.

10 Beaches

Side's glorious western beach *(right)* is full of high-end resort hotels and leisure facilities. At the smaller beaches on the eastern side, guides offer camel tours of the ruins.

Slave-Trading

In the 2nd century BC, Side became a haven for both pirates and slave-traders, who turned the town into an infamous market where slaves from North Africa were bought and sold. After a number of unsuccessful assaults, the Romans eventually gained control of Side in 70 BC. Slavery was an accepted part of Roman culture, and the trade is thought to have continued under their control.

TOP10 Alanya

With its dramatic rocky promontory, Alanya has attracted settlers for centuries. Defensive walls first erected by the Ancient Greeks were extended to their present length after Sultan Alaeddin Keykubat I conquered the city in 1221. A magnificent winter residence was constructed upon the summit, and although the sultan's palace has long since crumbled, the castle walls remain. Nowadays, Alanya is one of the coast's most popular resorts – a magnet for tourists, who flock to the town for its beaches, shopping and nightlife.

James Dean Dance Bar

🕐 Save yourself a long walk to the castle by taking one of the half-hourly buses (10:15am–8:15pm) that depart from opposite the Tourist Information Centre.

🍴 If you choose to walk down from the castle, you will pass plenty of small cafés serving drinks and snacks along the road – most of them have glorious views from their shaded outdoor terraces.

• Map L5
• Alanya Tourist Information Centre: Dalmataş Cad 1; (0242) 513 12 40; www.alanya.com.tr
• Alanya Museum of Archaeology: Hilmibağci Sok, Saray Mah; (0242) 513 12 28; Open 9am–7pm Tue–Sun; Adm

Top 10 Features

1. Alanya Castle
2. Red Tower
3. Süleymaniye Mosque
4. Alanya Museum
5. Byzantine Church
6. Damlataş Cave
7. Shipyard (Tersane)
8. Beaches
9. Nightlife
10. Shopping

Red Tower
This imposing red-brick octagonal tower *(above)* was built by the Syrian architect Ebu Ali in 1226. It could shelter up to 2,000 people in times of danger and supply them with water from the great cistern at its central core. Today, its ground floor houses an ethnographic museum.

Süleymaniye Mosque
Tucked away down a leafy street beneath the castle walls, this historic mosque *(right)* is another of Sultan Keykubat's many contributions to the town.

Alanya Castle
Occupying a commanding position high above the sea, the inner castle was built with defensive double walls snaking for 6.5 km (4 miles) over the rocky outcrop *(main image)*.

In Roman times, Alanya was known as Coracesium – opinions vary as to the name's origin.

Alanya Museum
4 The museum brings together a wide range of locally sourced artifacts, from Roman mosaics *(above)* to a display of historic farming tools. One of the oldest exhibits is an inscription in the Phoenician language dating back to the 6th century BC.

Byzantine Church
5 Used as a mosque during Selçuk times, this small church within the castle walls dates back to the Byzantine period. Badly in need of restoration, the church is presently closed to visitors.

Damlataş Cave
6 Filled with colourful stalactites and stalagmites, this broad cavern lies some 50 m (164 ft) beneath Alanya's rocky outcrop. Sufferers of rheumatism and asthma can visit the cave outside tourist opening hours to benefit from its high level of humidity and unusually high percentage of carbon dioxide *(see p98)*.

Shipyard (Tersane)
7 The shipyard's arches *(above)* lead into five interconnected chambers 44 m (144 ft) deep, that were used for the construction of wooden warships during the period of Selçuk rule that began in 1227 with Keykubat I.

Alanya After Keykubat

After the death of Sultan Alaeddin Keykubat I in 1237 there was no clear succession, and in the ensuing power vacuum Alanya's fortunes waned. From 1293 to 1427 it was ruled intermittently by the Karamanoğlu Dynasty, who eventually sold it to the Mameluks of Egypt for 5,000 gold pieces. Sultan Mehmet II brought it under Ottoman control in 1471, and from then it remained a part of the province of Anatolia.

Nightlife
9 The town has a truly vibrant nightlife scene, most of which is focused on a compact but intense quarter of bars and clubs by the old harbour.

Beaches
8 There are two lovely long stretches of golden sand – East Beach and Cleopatra Beach *(below)*, named after the Egyptian queen who reputedly once bathed there.

Shopping
10 Alanya is packed with shops and stalls selling everything from beach toys to priceless jewellery. If you feel like haggling, try the harbour bazaar or the Friday bazaar.

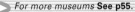

For more museums See p55.

TOP 10 Marmaris

With a population that swells from 30,000 to 300,000 in high season, Marmaris is a far cry from the humble fishing village it once was. Package tourists were first drawn to its long beach, natural harbour and stunning location during the late 1970s. Subsequent development has swamped much of the old town, leaving just the castle and a few narrow streets intact. With a high-class marina, the coast's best nightlife, irresistible shopping opportunities and countless bars, cafés and restaurants, it's no surprise that tourists continue to throng here.

View of Marmaris

Top 10 Features

1. Bar Street Nightlife
2. Castle and Museum
3. Old Town (Kaleiçi)
4. Grand Bazaar
5. Long Beach
6. Netsel Marina
7. Bazaar Hamam
8. Dolphin Therapy Centre
9. Günnücek National Park
10. Boat Trips

🔗 There's so much competition for day trips and water sports that it's well worth taking the time to investigate exactly what's on offer along the seafront before you strike a deal with one of the ever-eager boat touts.

💡 Take advantage of the two-for-one early evening drinks deals offered by most clubs and bars; prices revert to their usual extortionate rates later.

• Map C4
• Tourist Information Centre: İskele Meydani 2; (0252) 412 10 35; Open 8:30am–6pm Mon–Fri, 10am–5pm Sat–Sun; www.marmaris.org
• Marmaris Castle and Archaeological Museum: Kaleiçi; Map P6; (0252) 412 14 59; Open 9am–7pm Tue–Sun

1 Bar Street Nightlife

A single narrow street in the old town *(above)* hosts the south coast's wildest nightlife scene; clubs with open-air arenas thunder out the latest pop hits.

2 Castle and Museum

Founded in the 16th century, the castle *(below)* is now home to the town's museum. It sits on a low hill first used for a citadel in the 3rd century BC.

3 Old Town (Kaleiçi)

The Old Town's warren of winding streets is a delight to explore. Most of the white-washed Ottoman-era houses *(main image)* have been converted into restaurants, shops and bars; nonetheless, the area has managed to retain much of its period charm.

Grand Bazaar

This vast labyrinth of brightly lit shops and stalls *(above)* may lack old-world atmosphere, but it makes up for it in sheer quantity.

Long Beach

Despite its great length, Long Beach is always overcrowded in high season; yet it remains a focal point for tourists who sunbathe by day and fill the countless beachfront bars and restaurants by night.

Netsel Marina

With its pleasant mall of exclusive boutiques and every conceivable facility, Netsel Marina *(above)*, one of the best marinas on the coast, is frequented by wealthy yachters.

Dolphin Therapy Centre

The dolphinarium is used principally for a course of anti-stress treatment, but tourists may spend short periods with the three specially trained dolphins.

Bazaar Hamam

Tucked away in the bazaar opposite the Old Mosque, this small, century-old mixed-sex *hamam* is used by both locals and tourists. Relax in its marble-clad interior and enjoy being steamed, scrubbed and massaged.

Nelson's Visit

One of Marmaris' most illustrious guests was rear admiral Sir Horatio Nelson (1758–1805), who sheltered his small squadron of 13 ships in the town's harbour during the summer of 1798 before boldly attacking the huge fleet that Napoleon Bonaparte (1769–1821) had anchored at Aboukir Bay on the Egyptian coast. Nelson's surprise offensive on the evening of 1 August 1798 and the subsequent days of fighting wiped out the French navy and reversed the balance of power in the Mediterranean.

Günnücek National Park

Just a short walk south of the town centre, this forested park with its secluded bays and picnic areas is perfect for those in need of an escape from all the hustle and bustle of Marmaris.

Boat Trips

Countless traditional-style *gulet* and other tour boats *(above)* line the seafront, offering diving trips and cheap all-inclusive day trips to local islands, caves and beaches. There are daily ferries to Rhodes.

For more on marinas See pp42–3.

⬛10 Fethiye

It was the ancient Lycians who, in the 5th century BC, first identified the sheltered bay at what is now Fethiye as the ideal spot for a harbour. They built the city of Telmessos on the surrounding hillside and many of their remarkable tombs can still be seen. The name Fethiye is a tribute to local pilot Fethi Bey, a pioneering Turkish aviator, whose statue stands beside the harbour. Holidaymakers, particularly the British, have been enjoying Fethiye's attractive blend of relaxed local life and visitor-friendly facilities since the 1980s; many have returned to settle here.

The ruins of Fethiye Castle

🕐 For local news and events, pick up a copy of the English-language newspaper *Land of Lights*, which is distributed free in most bars, hotels and restaurants.

🍴 Just beneath Fethiye's ruined castle, the Kale Park restaurant *(see p84)* has great food and the best views in town.

• Map E5
• Tourist Information Centre: Iskele Meydani 1; (0252) 614 15 27; Open 8am–8pm Mon–Fri, 10am–7pm Sat–Sun; www.fethiye.net
• Fethiye Museum: Off Atatürk Cad; (0252) 614 11 50; Open 9am–5pm Tue–Sun; Adm

Top 10 Features

1. Amyntas' Tomb
2. Old Turkish Baths
3. Telmessos Theatre
4. Fethiye Castle
5. Çalış Beach
6. Bazaar
7. Fethiye Museum
8. Nightlife
9. Twelve Islands Boat Tour
10. Kaya Köyü

Amyntas' Tomb
Built for Amyntas, an ancient king of Telmessos, the grand tomb *(below)* cut into the cliffs high above the town has the façade of an Ionic temple, an image often used as a symbol of Fethiye.

Telmessos Theatre
Occupying a splendid spot facing the harbour, this ancient Hellenistic theatre wasn't uncovered until 1993, and is still in need of restoration. A focal point of ancient Telmessos, it could seat an audience of 5,000.

Old Turkish Baths
This 16th-century bath-house offers the rejuvenating delights of a classic Turkish steam bath, with traditional services such as scrub-downs and soap massages.

Fethiye Castle
Set high above the town, only the ruined walls remain of a Roman fort thought to have been renovated by the crusading Knights of Saint John in the 15th century.

Aside from tourism, Fethiye's main industry today is tomato production.

5 Çalış Beach

This 6-km (4-mile) stretch of well-maintained beach *(above)* lies just north of town. Hotels and restaurants line the seafront.

6 Bazaar

Known as Paspatur, Fethiye's bazaar quarter is a pleasant warren of shaded streets packed with shops and stalls selling a range of wares from carpets to colourful spices *(right)* and the usual array of souvenirs.

7 Fethiye Museum

This informative museum features artifacts dating back to the Bronze Age, including a collection of promissory steles *(detail, right)* and treasures discovered at Tlos and Kaunos.

9 Twelve Islands Boat Tour

A popular day trip from Fethiye harbour, passengers travel in wooden *gulets* to Tersane Island, the five islands around Yassica Island, and several smaller islands and bays. There are frequent swimming stops and lunch is included.

10 Kaya Köyü

The intriguing ruined buildings of Kaya Köyü *(left),* a predominantly Greek-Christian town that was abandoned in 1923, lie a short drive south of Fethiye. It's a fascinating place to explore, and there are plenty of atmospheric restaurants and *pensions* nearby.

8 Nightlife

Fethiye's nightlife scene is centred upon Paspatur Caddesi, where quirky bars and clubs have found their niche among the characterful buildings of the Old Town. Music ranges from live rock to popular Turkish.

The British are Coming

The British have been visiting Fethiye on package tours since the 1980s, but it wasn't until the late 1990s that they began buying homes here. By 2005, it was estimated that 10,000 apartments and houses had been sold to British buyers, many of whom decided to settle permanently. Retirees are the most common group, but Fethiye is also home to a number of British-run businesses. Since the financial crisis, British buying has tailed off, but Russian and Arab buyers have taken up the slack.

🔟 Kaş

Kaş's sheltered natural harbour has attracted settlers for millennia, but little more of the ancient site remains than the theatre, some rock tombs and a few scattered sarcophagi. An estimated 250,000 tourists visit Kaş each year, yet despite that, it has retained its small-town charm. By day, adventurous types can sample diving, paragliding and kayaking, while those more inclined to relaxation can simply chill out on a seafront swimming platform. At dusk, Kaş's narrow streets come alive, as the main square fills with promenading locals and tourists.

Lion Tomb

🚤 Small boats run frequent shuttle services between the harbour and two pebble beaches just outside Kaş.

🍵 The laid-back tea gardens along Kaş's western seafront have their own rocky swimming platforms, with waiter service for sunbathers.

• Map F6
• Tourist Information Centre: Cumhuriyet Meydani 5; (0242) 836 12 38; Open 8:30am–6pm Mon–Fri

Top 10 Features

1. Lion Tomb
2. Doric Tomb
3. Cistern
4. Antiphellos Theatre
5. Shopping
6. Hellenistic Temple
7. Diving
8. Old Harbour
9. Boat Trips
10. Harbour Mosque

Doric Tomb
Illuminated at night, the impressive rock tombs above Kaş were chiselled out by the Lycians around the 5th century BC. The best example is the Doric Tomb *(above)*, a large, house-like chamber with an interior frieze depicting dancing female figures.

Lion Tomb

This famous Lycian pillar tomb measures 8 m (26 ft) in height. The sarcophagus is mounted on a two-tiered podium that stands at the top of a busy shopping street.

Cistern
The cistern was cut into the rock some 2,500 years ago. Originally designed for water storage, it was later used for preserving olive oil and vegetables.

Antiphellos Theatre
Dating back to the 4th century BC, this well-preserved theatre was built without a stage – typical of the early Hellenistic period. There are lovely sea views from the top *(left)*.

Kaş was built on the site of the ancient city of Antiphellos.

Shopping
5 Kaş's shopping scene comes alive around dusk, when it's cool enough to browse the colourful wares of the small shops that stay open till after midnight selling unique handmade crafts *(above)*.

Hellenistic Temple
6 Although experts agree that the ruin just off Necip Bay Caddesi is that of a Hellenistic temple, little else is known about it. The remnants of its walls consist of massive, neatly shaped blocks.

Diving
7 Home to no fewer than 16 diving clubs, Kaş is considered one of the south coast's best diving centres *(above)*. Popular dive sites include wrecks, reefs and underwater caves and canyons.

Old Harbour
8 Kaş's harbour *(main image)* occupies a lovely spot in the town centre and offers basic facilities for yachts. The modern 450-berth Kaş marina lies just outside of town.

Boat Trips
9 Tour boats depart daily for the sunken ruins of Kekova, as do organized sea-kayaking tours. There are also regular ferries to the nearby island of Meis.

Harbour Mosque
10 The Harbour Mosque *(above)* is perhaps the most interesting of Kaş's three mosques. Tourists can view the interior outside prayer times.

Lycian Tombs

There are four easily distinguishable types of Lycian tomb. The earliest are known as "pillar tombs" and consist of sarcophagi mounted on rectangular stone pillars. "Temple tombs" mimicked the façade of a temple in a rock face, and have a door to a burial chamber within. "House tombs" were built to resemble houses with two or three floors. The most common tombs are the sarcophagi found throughout Lycia, which consist of a base, a burial chamber and an arched lid.

Left **Ruined Byzantine church inside Alanya Castle** Right **Selçuk inscriptions, Antalya Museum**

⁹⁰₁₀ Moments in History

1 546 BC: Persian invasion
The Persians, under the command of King Cyrus II (576–530 BC), add Pamphylia and Lycia to their vast empire. They remain in control there for over 200 years.

2 334 BC: Alexander the Great
The legendary commander marches eastwards from his native Macedonia on a campaign that brings about the collapse of the Persian empire. After Alexander's death in 323 BC the region is divided between his generals, and a period of Greek influence ensues.

3 133 BC: Anatolia Becomes a Province of the Roman Empire
Knowing that he will die without an heir and anxious to avoid civil war, Attalus III of Pergamon (170–133 BC) bequeaths his kingdom to the Romans. They establish the province of Asia, with its capital first at Pergamon and later at Ephesus.

4 AD 330: Founding of the Byzantine Empire
Nearly three decades after the Romans adopt Christianity as their official religion, Emperor Constantine founds the Byzantine Empire when he consecrates its new capital, Constantinople, on the site of former Byzantium.

Alexander the Great

5 1068: Invasion of the Selçuk Muslims
Expanding westwards from Persia, the Selçuk muslims under Alparslan (1029–72) invade the Byzantine Empire, establishing principalities along the south and west coasts.

6 1453: The Ottomans take Constantinople
Following gradual territorial incursions by the Ottomans over the previous century, Mehmed II (1432–81) captures Constantinople, making it his new capital and renaming it Istanbul.

7 1919: The Treaty of Sèvres
Following the defeat of the Ottoman Empire in World War I, Greece is given control of much of the western Turkish coast. This sparks the Turkish War of Independence (1919–23), whose Greek campaign (also known as the Greco-Turkish War) resulted in a massive Greek-and-Turkish population exchange in 1923.

The Siege of Constantinople in 1453 (16th-century fresco)

Preceding pages **Visitors strolling through the picturesque streets of Kalkan**

8 1923: Formation of the Turkish Republic

Signed in 1923, The Treaty of Lausanne annuls the Treaty of Sèvres and leads to the recognition of the new Republic of Turkey. Mustafa Kemal Atatürk is elected president and implements the sweeping reforms that will transform Turkey into a modern, democratic and, above all, secular nation.

President Mustafa Kemal Atatürk in 1923

9 1980s: Tourism Boom

Long considered an exotic destination, Turkey begins to attract an ever-growing number of tourists following the Tourism Encouragement Law of 1982 and extensive investment in infrastructure. Kuşadası, Marmaris and Bodrum develop most rapidly, and the number of tourists visiting Turkey annually escalates from one million in 1974 to over 25 million in 2008.

10 2005: Invitation to Join the European Union

Despite significant reservations from within the European Union, Turkey is invited to begin EU accession negotiations in October 2005. (It had first applied to join in 1987.) The ongoing discussions have been slowed by a variety of factors, and although acceptance is possible as early as 2013, observers consider it unlikely to happen before 2020.

Top 10 Great Leaders

1 Alexander the Great (356–323 BC)
This legendary leader forced the Persians out of Turkey.

2 Emperor Constantine (AD 280–337)
The first Roman emperor to adopt Christianity, Constantine founded Constantinople.

3 Sultan Keykubat (1190–1237)
The renowned Selçuk leader built the great fortresses and palaces at Alanya and Konya.

4 Sultan Mehmet II (1432–81)
Also called "The Conqueror", Mehmet II took Constantinople from the Byzantines in 1453.

5 Sultan Abdul Hamid II (1842–1918)
Hamid II drew up the Ottoman Empire's first constitution in 1876 but never implemented it.

6 Enver Paşa (1881–1922)
War minister and commander-in-chief during World War I, Enver Paşa took the decision to join the Central Powers.

7 Mustafa Kemal Atatürk (1881–1938)
This revered leader founded and became first president of the Republic of Turkey.

8 Ismet Inönü (1884–1973)
Inönü became president after Atatürk's death in 1938.

9 Celal Bayar (1883–1986)
Bayar became Turkey's third president in 1950 when his People's Republican Party won Turkey's first free elections.

10 Turgut Özal (1927–93)
Prime minister and president from 1983 to 1993, Özal fostered capitalism through privatization.

Left **The Lycian Way near Çıralı** Right Mount Olympos, Beydağları National Park

Areas of Natural Beauty

Unspoiled Beaches
Despite the overdevelopment that has blighted parts of Turkey's southwestern coast, a number of beaches remain untouched, thanks to the endangered loggerhead turtles that nest there. Patara *(see p80)* and İztuzu *(see p70)* beaches both have long stretches of fine sand backed by nothing more than dunes. Çıralı beach *(see p40)* and the tiny Kaputaş beach *(see p82)* are also sublime.

The Lycian Way
Marked in 2000 by British walker Kate Clow, this walking trail that extends over 500 km (300 miles) passes through the heart of the Beydağları National Park. The landscapes range from spectacular snow-capped mountains and dramatic gorges to miles of idyllic beaches and villages untouched by tourism *(see pp20–21)*.

Saklıkent Gorge
This deep limestone gorge is Turkey's longest. One-fifth of its 20-km (13-mile) length is accessible between April and September, when water levels are low enough to allow those with canyoning equipment to penetrate further into its recesses. Visitors must pass through the icy waters of an underground river near the entrance before continuing into the gorge *(see p80)*.

Saklıkent Gorge

Chimaera
Accessed by a steep track from the car park below it, the Chimaera's flames, flickering from a rocky hillside within the Beydağları National Park, provide an entrancing sight for visitors. Fuelled by natural gas from deep below the ground, the phenomenon – said by some to be the origin of the myth of the Chimera – is at its most impressive after dark *(see p88)*.

Beydağları National Park
Encompassing a swathe of mountainous land stretching for 90 km (56 miles) south from Antalya to the tip of the peninsula below Adrasan, the Beydağları National Park shelters a broad diversity of wildlife and is traversed by the Lycian Way. The only coastal spots to benefit from its protection are Olympos and Çirali, where development has been kept to a minimum *(see p88)*.

Göynük Canyon
Göynük's 10-km (6-mile) canyon narrows to as little as 6 m (20 ft) wide in places. It features smooth limestone walls similar to those at Saklıkent, but has larger pools that must be swum across – the water temperature is usually around 8–10°C. ✆ *Map H5*

7 Waterfalls

The waterfalls at Kurşunlu *(see p90)* and Düden are among the most spectacular in the region, and are at their best in spring when the rivers are swollen by melt-water. Düden's upper waterfalls lie just north of Antalya; its lower waterfalls cascade from a clifftop into the sea east of the city. ◈ *Map H4 (Düden)*

Düden Waterfalls

8 The Turkish Lake District

Eğirdir *(see p90)* and Beyşehir are the largest of several shallow lakes that lie between the Taurus Mountains in a picturesque region known as the Turkish Lake District. The small lakeside town of Eğirdir provides a convenient base for the many outdoor activities on offer. ◈ *Map K3 (Beyşehir)*

9 Köprülü Canyon National Park

Covering 36,000 hectares (139 sq miles) forested with cypress, pine, oak and cedar trees, Köprülü Canyon National Park is home to wolves, boars, bears and a large variety of bird species. At its core lies Köprülü Canyon, a great fissure in the limestone rock up to 100 m (63 ft) deep and 400 m (250 ft) wide in places *(see p97)*.

10 Dim Cave

A site of stunning underground natural beauty, Dim Cave lies in the mountains east of Alanya. It comprises a series of caverns filled with eerie rock formations that were sculpted from limestone by millions of years of erosion. A 350-m (1,148-ft) walkway leads visitors into the depths of the mountain. At the end of the cave there is a small lake *(see p99)*.

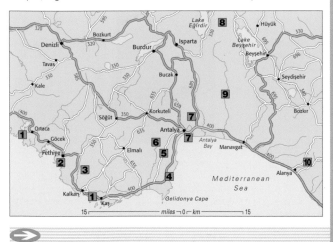

Left **Whirling dervishes at the Mevlâna Festival** Right **Camel-wrestling in Selçuk**

TOP 10 Festivals

1 Ramazan (Ramadan)
Ramazan (Ramadan) – the ninth month of the Islamic lunar calendar – is a period when Muslims throughout the world fast between dawn and dusk. Intended to cleanse the soul, the fasting is broken at sunset, when crowds of people gather at mosques and outdoor stalls to eat and drink. Because the lunar calendar is 11 days shorter than the standard solar one, the dates of *Ramazan* vary from year to year.

2 Camel-Wrestling Festival, Selçuk
This ancient sport takes place every January in Selçuk and the surrounding area. It involves two colourfully attired bull camels somewhat half-heartedly butting each other until one backs down. The event attracts large numbers of spectators, who eagerly gamble on the outcome. ✎ *Map B2*

3 Marmaris Maritime and Spring Festival
This vibrant festival lasts for five days in May. Events include yacht racing, beach volleyball, traditional music performances, parades and sand-sculpting competitions. It all culminates in a weekend of tug-of-war and *gulet* racing, and a picnic in the park. ✎ *Map C4 • www.marmarisfestival.com*

4 Ephesus International Festival of Culture
Each May, Ephesus and Selçuk host a festival to celebrate Turkish culture and history. Dance troupes and music groups from around the country perform on the stage of the great Roman theatre. ✎ *Map A2*

5 Alanya International Tourism and Art Festival
Also in May, Alanya's festival consists mostly of classical concerts performed by Turkish and international orchestras in the Red Tower *(see p24)* and the Town Hall. ✎ *Map L5*

6 Aspendos Opera and Ballet Festival
Every June, audiences of up to 2,500 pack into the ancient theatre *(see p97)* for shows by Turkish and international opera and ballet troupes. ✎ *Map J4 • www.aspendosfestival.gov.tr*

Poster for the Aspendos Opera and Ballet Festival

7 International Lycian Festival, Kaş
Held over a long week-end at the end of June, this entertaining event takes place at Kaş's Hellenistic Theatre and beside the harbour. Events include displays of paragliding, folk dancing, cookery demonstrations, swimming and boating competitions and art exhibitions. ✎ *Map F6*

Dates for Ramazan: 20 Jul–18 Aug (2012); 9 Jul–7 Aug (2013); 28 Jun–27 Jul (2014)

8 Oil-Wrestling Festival, Elmalı

Turkey is famous for its wrestling culture and holds many organized events throughout the country. The Elmalı festival takes place at the beginning of August and features the traditional spectacle of participants dressed in leather shorts and drenched in olive oil, to make them as slippery as possible. ◉ *Map F5*

Oil-wrestling Festival, Elmalı

9 Antalya Golden Orange Film Festival

Film enthusiasts flock to Antalya every October for the country's most important festival of Turkish films and documentaries. The International Eurasia Film Festival runs concurrently and is open to directors from all over the world. ◉ *Map H5* • *www.aksav.org.tr*

10 Mevlâna Whirling Dervish Festival, Konya

The Mevlâna Whirling Dervish Festival commemorates the death of the poet and mystic Mevlâna, founder of the Sufi brotherhood, who died in Konya on 17 December 1273. Each December, followers from around the world converge on Konya for two weeks of Dervish dancing that culminates with a frenetic celebration of Mevlâna's "wedding" with Allah on the anniversary of his death. ◉ *Map M2*

Top 10 Traditional Instruments

1 Tar
Similar to a lute, the *tar* is a stringed instrument with a thin membrane stretched over its body.

2 Zurna
The *zurna* is a wooden pipe that widens towards the bottom, producing a range of loud sounds.

3 Kaval
This wooden flute may have been used by shepherds to direct their flocks.

4 Tulum
Tulum is the Turkish name for a bagpipe commonly used throughout the Balkans.

5 Kaşik
These percussive wooden spoons are played back to back in a pair; the best are made from light yellow boxwood.

6 Darbuka
This large drum held under one arm and played with the hands once had a therapeutic role; its rhythmic beats were used to treat high blood pressure and heart conditions.

7 Saz
Part of the *bağlama* family, the *saz* is a stringed instrument with a long, narrow neck.

8 Mey
This double-reed woodwind instrument like an oboe is thought to have been invented some 3,000 years ago.

9 Bağlama
The *bağlama* is a bulbous wooden stringed instrument with a long, narrow neck. It has been played throughout Turkey for centuries.

10 Kabak Kemane
Traditionally fashioned from a gourd, this three-stringed violin is played with a long bow.

Left **Ölüdeniz beach** Right **İztuzu beach**

Beaches

Turunç Beach
1 Turunç is a peaceful tourist village hidden away in a secluded bay whose small sandy beach is surrounded by wooded hills. Though it's usually packed with umbrellas, the beach and the shallow turquoise sea still make a picturesque sight, attracting both yachters and holiday-makers in search of a quiet break. ◈ *Map C5*

İztuzu Beach
2 Also known as Turtle Beach, this superb 5-km (3-mile) stretch of sand spanning the mouth of the Dalyan Strait is completely undeveloped thanks to the endangered loggerhead turtles that nest here. Surrounded by forested hills, its shallow, transparent waters are perfect for children. ◈ *Map D5*

Sarıgerme Beach
3 This lovely broad white sandy beach *(see also p71)* is surrounded by unobtrusive 4- and 5-star hotel complexes that are half-hidden by woods and bushes. To get to the beach,

Sarıgerme beach

visitors must walk or catch a shuttle, as cars are required to park some distance away. The modest admission charge is used to keep the beach clean and tidy. ◈ *Map D5 • Adm*

Ölüdeniz Beach
4 The thousands of paragliders who take to the skies above Ölüdeniz every season have by far the best view of its famous beach *(see also p79)*. The most heavily photographed section lies to the west of the overcrowded resort beside the blue lagoon; for access to this part of the beach visitors must pay an entry fee, which also allows them the use of a sun lounger. ◈ *Map E5 • Adm*

Patara Beach
5 Backed by windswept sand dunes covering the ruins of the once-great city of Patara *(see p83)*, this is another fantastic expanse of golden sand saved from development by nesting loggerheads. ◈ *Map E6 • Adm*

Kaputaş Beach
6 Trapped between steep cliffs, this tiny beach, with its bright blue waters and golden sand, attracts visitors from miles around, including passengers from the *gulet* tour boats that stop here for swimming breaks. ◈ *Map E6*

Çıralı Beach
7 Shared by the adjacent settlements of Olympos and Çıralı *(see p90)*, this fine pebble

9 Side Beach

Side has two excellent beaches. The safe, shallow waters at West Beach tend to attract the greatest number of tourists, while the windswept dunes of East Beach are a little wilder and generally quieter. This is the only spot along the coast where camel rides are offered. ◎ Map K5

10 Cleopatra Beach

Named after the celebrated Egyptian queen, who is reputed to have bathed here, Cleopatra Beach lies to the west of the rocky peninsula that marks the southernmost point of the city of Alanya (see pp24–5). It's an attractive, sandy strip that gets very busy in high season and backs onto an unbroken line of hotels and restaurants. ◎ Map L6

Camels on Side beach

beach – like Patara and İztuzu, home to nesting turtles – is protected from development by its inclusion in Beydağlari National Park (see p88). It is an idyllic spot with clear waters, and there are tranquil, palm-shaded outdoor restaurants nearby. ◎ Map H6

8 Konyaaltı Beach

Stretching away from the city towards the distant Taurus mountain range, Konyaaltı beach is the seaside centrepiece of the international resort city of Antalya (see pp8–9). The famous pebble beach has a Blue Flag award for cleanliness – despite the large number of tourists who use it in high season. ◎ Map H5

Konyaaltı beach

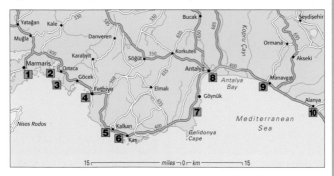

For more on beaches **See p82.**

41

Left **Port Göcek Marina** Centre **Ece Saray Marina Resort, Fethiye** Right **Finike Marina**

🔟 Marinas

1 Bodrum Marina
Bodrum's medieval castle guards the entrance to Bodrum Marina – a popular destination for yachters keen to explore this atmospheric town *(see p108)*. The 475-berth marina has all the usual facilities, including shops, restaurants, a clinic, a pharmacy, maintenance services and 24-hour security. ⊗ *Map A4 • (0252) 316 18 60 • www.miltabodrummarina.com*

2 Netsel Marina, Marmaris
An hour-and-a-half's drive from Dalaman International Airport and conveniently located next to the old town *(see pp26–7)*, this well-equipped marina with space for up to 750 boats is among the largest on the coast. It has a boutique shopping mall, bars, restaurants, laundry services and free showers for guests. ⊗ *Map Q5 • (0252) 412 27 08 • www.netselmarina.com*

3 Port Göcek Marina, Göcek
Göcek may be small, but it's a busy yachting destination, with four marinas catering to the constant flow of boats. The high-class option is the 380-berth Port Göcek Marina, which shares a private beach with the 5-star Swissotel Göcek *(see p126)*. There are Wi-Fi and cable-TV connections, and you can have breakfast delivered to your boat. ⊗ *Map D5 • (0252) 645 15 20 • www.portgocek.com*

4 Ece Saray Marina, Fethiye
Fethiye's marina is large – it can accommodate 450 boats. Located near the town centre, its facilities are first-rate, including a supermarket, a laundry service, immaculate bathrooms, a hotel *(see p127)* and a smart restaurant *(see p84)* which hosts a garden barbecue most weekends. ⊗ *Map E5 • (0252) 612 50 05 • www.ecesaray.net*

Netsel Marina, Marmaris

Kalkan Marina

5 Overlooked by Kalkan's laid-back seafront bars and restaurants, this small marina with around 80 berths offers a basic range of services. Fuel is available at 6pm daily, there are laundry and washing facilities, and guests can use the marina's canoes free of charge. ◎ *Map E6* • *(0242) 844 31 31*

Kaş Marina

6 Yachters used to moor at Kaş harbour, before the opening of the 472-berth Kaş Marina in May 2011. Located to the west of Kaş centre, the new marina offers an exemplary range of services, including heliport, swimming pool and spa centre. ◎ *Map F6* • *www.kasmarina.com.tr*

Finike Marina

7 Located in the heart of this pleasant seaside town, Finike's large marina has a yacht club with a bar where yachters gather for organized events. Also on offer are Wi-Fi; a fuel station; a maintenance yard; WC, shower and laundry facilities; and a swimming pool. ◎ *Map G6* • *(0242) 855 50 30* • *www.seturmarinas.com*

Kemer Marina

8 At the foot of the low, forested hills that encircle the pleasant resort of Kemer, this 230-berth marina offers a full range of maintenance services including carpentry and sail repairs. Dance classes, language lessons and cinema screenings are among the activities on offer. ◎ *Map H5* • *(0242) 814 14 90* • *www.kemerturkizmarina.com*

Kemer Marina

Çelebi Marina, Antalya

9 South of Çelebi city centre, Çelebi Marina has superb modern facilities including a children's playground, a swimming pool, a yacht club with a library and games room and a top-notch restaurant. ◎ *Map H5* • *(0242) 259 32 59* • *www.celebimarina.com*

Alanya Marina

10 Alanya's smart marina has a capacity of around 300 boats. It's situated just outside the city, so the free shuttle bus saves a long walk to the centre. The marina itself has a bar and restaurant, a supermarket, a yacht chandlery, a fitness centre, tennis courts and more. ◎ *Map L5* • *(0242) 512 12 34* • *www.alanyamarina.com.tr*

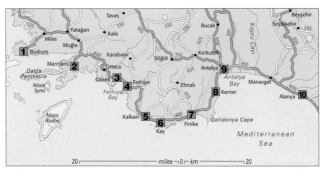

Left **Tour boats from Alanya** Centre **Sunken ruins of Kekova** Right **View of Meis from Kaş**

🔟 Boat Trips

1 Üçağiz and Kaş to Kekova
The sunken ruins at Kekova *(see p21)* are the destination of boat trips from all over the region. The quickest way to reach them is by fishing boat from Üçağiz (trips last around an hour). Alternatively, larger boats depart from Kaş harbour for day trips that include Kekova. Dragoman Tours organize kayaking trips to Kekova from Kaş. ✎ *Map F6*
• www.dragoman-turkey.com

2 Dalyan River Trips
An endless procession of small boats chugs up and down the Dalyan Strait in high season, ferrying day-tripping tourists between the mud baths at Köyceğiz Lake *(see p69)*, past the rock tombs cut into the cliffs, and on to İztuzu beach and the coastal ruins of Kaunos *(see p70)*. ✎ *Map D5*

Dalyan river trips

3 Alanya's Caves
Small wooden fishing boats carrying up to eight passengers run hour-long trips around Alanya's rocky promontory, stopping off at the ancient shipyard, Tersane *(see p25)*, Pirate's Cave *(see p100)*, Phosphorous Cave and Cleopatra Beach *(see p25)*. Larger *gulets* depart from the harbour on day trips. ✎ *Map L5*

4 Twelve Islands
Double-decker wooden *gulets* accommodating from 50 to 150 passengers run this popular day trip from Fethiye harbour, departing between 10 and 11am each morning and returning in the early evening. There are several swimming opportunities during the day, including one at Tersane Island – once inhabited by Greeks – as well as stops at several smaller islands with idyllic bays. Lunch is included and the boats have onboard bars. ✎ *Map E5*

5 Kaş to Meis
Surprisingly, the large island just a short distance from Kaş *(see pp30–31)* is Greek territory. Known as Meis or Kastellorizo, it has a population of around 450 and – like many islands in the Dodecanese, of which it is the smallest – a scattering of Ottoman-era ruins. The trip from Kaş harbour takes 45 minutes and is often made by long-term visitors to renew their 90-day Turkish tourist visas. ✎ *Map F6*

Traditionally, a gulet is a two-masted wooden sailing vessel from the southwest coast of Turkey. Today, most of them run on diesel.

Gulet moored in a bay west of Datça

Datça to Knidos

Day trips from Datça can be made with fishing boats or *gulets*. The boats follow the peninsula to Knidos *(see p68)*, where tourists have the chance to explore the ruins. There are several swimming spots at secluded bays and dinner is provided. 🚩 *Map B5*

Kemer to Phaselis

The picturesque coastal ruins of Phaselis can be visited on a small chartered boat from Kemer harbour; it's a 2-hour trip. Alternatively, you can take a day trip with a larger group on a *gulet* that also stops at isolated bays for swimming breaks, with lunch on board included. 🚩 *Map H5*

Gemiler Beach to Aya Nikola Island

Aya Nikola lies in a sheltered bay, just a short boat trip away from Gemiler Beach. Local fishermen drop tourists at the island; once there, they can picnic and explore the ruins of a chapel and several Lycian tombs before returning to the beach. 🚩 *Map E5*

Manavgat Falls

There are plenty of boats at Manavgat waiting to ferry passengers upriver to Manavgat Falls. Despite their lack of height, the volume of water gushing down is quite a spectacle, and the trip itself is pleasant. 🚩 *Map K5*

Marmaris to Rhodes

Anyone craving a change of scenery can board a catamaran (1 hour) or car ferry (2 hours) from Marmaris to Rhodes; both types of vessel usually depart daily at 9am, returning at 4pm. As with Meis, the trip is also a convenient way to renew 90-day Turkish tourist visas. 🚩 *Map C5*

View of Aya Nikola from Gemiler Beach

Left **Lycian house tombs, Tlos** Centre **Harpy Tomb, Xanthos** Right **The theatre at Ephesus**

🔟 Ancient Ruins

Ephesus
Capital of the Roman province of Asia, Ephesus was once the second largest city in the Roman Empire, after Rome itself. Although its spectacular Temple of Artemis – considered one of the Seven Wonders of the Ancient World – has been lost, much has survived, including a huge theatre, the grand Library of Celsus and a complex of mansions replete with murals and mosaics *(see pp14–15)*.

Aphrodisias
Partially hidden beneath the village of Geyre until the early 1960s, the remains of this great ancient city have since been exposed. Named after the Greek goddess of love, Aphrodite, its surviving structures include the remains of a temple to her, a monumental gateway (Tetrapylon), a stadium for 30,000 spectators and baths built in honour of the Emperor Hadrian *(see p108)*.

Tlos
Against a scenic backdrop of distant mountains, Tlos occupies a hilltop site first settled as early as 2000 BC. There are numerous Lycian house tombs carved into the rocky hillside above a large Roman stadium and theatre. On top of the hill are the ruined walls of an Ottoman fortress *(see p82)*.

Xanthos
During the 2nd century BC, Xanthos was the powerful capital of Lycia, and it continued to be an important settlement during the Roman era. A number of imposing Lycian pillar tombs stand proud of the scattered ruins. One bears the longest known inscription in the ancient Lycian language; another, the Harpy Tomb, is decorated with splendid marble reliefs. There are also Roman and Byzantine remains. The site was granted World Heritage status in 1988 *(see p80)*.

Arykanda
The founders of Arykanda built their settlement upon a series of five large terraces cut into a steep, rocky hillside. Its most significant ruins date from the Roman era, including temples, a number of rock tombs, several bath houses and a half-size theatre with sweeping views *(see p90)*.

Monumental gateway, Aphrodisias

Phaselis

6 These attractively situated ruins occupy a small peninsula that was supplied with water by an aqueduct during Roman times. Founded in the Lycian period, Phaselis became one of the region's key trading ports. Visitors can access the site by road or sea *(see p90)*.

Termessos

7 Founded upon a remote hilltop around the 6th century BC, Termessos developed into a powerful city that was granted autonomy by the Roman Empire. It has some impressive rock tombs, in particular the Tomb of Alcetas. Another highlight is the dramatic clifftop theatre *(see pp12–13)*.

Relief on rock, Tomb of Alcetas, Termessos

Perge

8 This ancient capital of Pamphylia was saved from destruction in 333 BC when its leaders wisely treated Alexander the Great and his invading army as honoured guests rather than enemies. It later developed into a great Roman city, and many

of its stunning statues and sarcophagi can be seen at Antalya's Archeological Museum *(see p89)*.

Aspendos

9 Aspendos is known above all for its incredibly well-preserved theatre, built in the 2nd century AD. Following the collapse of the Roman Empire, the theatre was restored by the Selçuks and used variously as an inn and as a palace. It has seating for up to 12,000 people, and still hosts regular performances, notably of the Aspendos International Opera and Ballet Festival each summer *(see p97)*.

Side

10 During Lycian and Roman times, the peninsula town of Side was a busy trading port. In the 1st and 2nd centuries BC, it was also a haven for pirates and slave-traders. Although only the foundations of the majority of its buildings remain, a number of major structures – such as the theatre, defensive walls and arches – are still standing to this day *(see pp22–3)*.

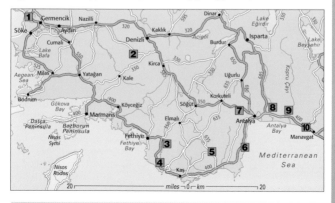

Left **Mehmet Paşa Mosque, Antalya** Right **Basilica of St John, Ephesus**

🔟 Places of Worship

1 Tekeli Mehmet Paşa Mosque, Antalya

Antalya's most important mosque was built in the 18th century in the Kaleiçi (old town) district. Its large central dome covers the prayer hall, which is entered via a smaller triple-domed structure *(see p9)*.

2 Eşrefoğlu Mosque, Beyşehir

Forty-two wooden pillars support the flat ceiling of this ancient mosque. Completed in 1299 during the Eşrefoğlu dynasty, its remarkable cedar-wood interior has survived against the odds. The secret of its longevity is thought to be the central *karlık* (snow well), which used to fill with snow and rain through a hole in the roof, keeping the air in the church humid and preventing the wood from drying out. ❦ *Map K3*

Yivli Minaret

Interior, Eşrefoğlu Mosque, Beyşehir

3 Church of St Nicholas, Demre

Thought to be the burial place of St Nicholas – the Bishop of Myra who metamorphosed into Santa Claus – this small 6th-century church was itself buried under alluvial silt until restoration began in the last century. The ceiling frescoes have been painstakingly restored and a service is held here once a year to celebrate St Nicholas Day on 6th December *(see p82)*.

4 Yivli Minaret, Antalya

Built during the reign of Sultan Alaeddin Keykubat (1219–38), this splendid 38-m (125-ft) minaret towers over Antalya's old town. It was originally covered with dark blue and turquoise tiles, of which just a few remain. Internal steps lead up to a balcony from which the call to prayer was once broadcast. Opposite is a 13th-century religious school *(medrese)*, now used as a textile bazaar *(see p9)*.

5 Süleymaniye Mosque, Alanya

Constructed in 1231, this plain, square-planned mosque was one of many new buildings erected in Alanya during the reign of Sultan Keykubat. Set on the rocky promontory a short distance below the fortress, the original structure was damaged by lightning in the 16th century and rebuilt soon after *(see p24)*.

6 Church of the Virgin Mary, Ephesus

Built on the ruins of a Roman temple around AD 500, this is considered the first church to have been dedicated to the Virgin Mary, who is believed by many to have lived in Ephesus in her later years. Ephesus gained historical significance in AD 431 as the venue for the Ecumenical Council's heated discussions about whether the Virgin Mary was *Christotokos* – bearer of Christ – or *Theotokos* – bearer of God. ✎ Map A2

7 St Philip Martyrium, Hierapolis

One of the twelve apostles, St Philip preached Christianity in Hierapolis and founded its first Christian community. In AD 87 he infuriated the governor by converting his wife, and was crucified upside-down for his troubles. The ruins of the Martyrium, a complex early-5th-century building arranged about a central octagonal structure, can be seen on a hilltop to the north of the site (see p19).

Korkut Minaret Mosque, Antalya

8 Korkut Mosque, Antalya

This unusual ruin stands on the site of a Roman temple that was subsequently converted to a Christian church. In the 13th century it became a Selçuk mosque before briefly reverting to a church under Cypriot King Peter I in 1361. Reinstated as a mosque by Prince Korkut (1470–1509), it remained open until 1896 when it lost the top of its minaret during a fire (see p9).

9 Af Kule Monastery, Fethiye

Now a dramatic ruin, this medieval monastery built into steep cliffs high above the sea is thought to have been the work of a lone monk who spent his life carving it into the rock with simple tools (see p83).

10 Basilica of St John, Ephesus

Thought to have been built in the 5th century over the grave of St John the Apostle, this basilica was later converted to a mosque. In the 14th century the building was destroyed by an earthquake. Since then, parts of it have been reconstructed; recent excavations have revealed a frescoed chapel. ✎ Map A2

Süleymaniye Mosque, Alanya

The Korkut (also known as the Kesik Minare, or "cut minaret")
mosque is named after Şehzade Korkut, son of Sultan Beyazıt II.

Left **Adaland Aquapark, Kuşadası** Centre **Chimaera** Right **Saklıkent Gorge**

Children's Activities

1 Adaland Aquapark, Kuşadası

This vast complex comprises an aqua ark with all the usual slides and pools, a dolphinarium and a sea park, where visitors can snorkel in a lagoon with tropical fish and even be lowered into a shark pool in a metal cage. ◈ *Çamlimani Mevkii • Map A2 • (0256) 618 12 52 • Open May–Oct: 10am–7pm daily • Adm • www.adaland.com*

2 Mud Baths, Dalyan

A mud bath from head to toe beside Köyceğiz Lake is likely to be the highlight of a boat trip from Dalyan for kids and adults alike. Wash it all off in the neighbouring thermal springs before chugging off to explore the coastal ruins at Kaunos, or stop for a swimming break at İztuzu beach. ◈ *Çamurlu Kaplıcası • Map D5 • (0252) 284 20 35 • Open 7:30am–6pm daily • Adm*

3 Atlantis Waterpark, Marmaris

Situated right in the heart of Marmaris, this well-equipped water park offers plenty of fun,

with facilities designed for kids of different ages. Free rubber rings are provided for the many slides, and there's also a wave pool. Anyone wanting to stay dry can opt for mini golf or a sunbed. ◈ *Uzunyali 203 Sok • Map C4 • (0252) 411 04 62 • Open May–Oct: 10am–6pm • Adm • www.marmariswaterpark.com*

4 Water Planet, Manavgat

Part of a holiday complex, this large water park has 27 slides, including the high-speed "Kamikaze" run and the "Multi Slide", where four people can slide side-by-side. There's also a pool for young children, rafting with artificial waves, bungee-jumping and mini golf. ◈ *Water Planet Holiday Village, Okurcalar Mevkii • Map K5 • (0242) 527 51 65 • Adm • www.waterplanet.com.tr*

5 Antalya Beach Park

Antalya's Beach Park is an extensive complex alongside Konyaaltı beach *(see p90)*. The main attractions are AquaLand – billed as Antalya's biggest water park – and DolphinLand, whose shows feature sea otters, dolphins and a white whale called Mila. There's also a paintballing area, not to mention beach bars, cafés and open-air restaurants aplenty. ◈ *Konyaaltı Beach • Map H5 • (0242) 249 09 08 • www.beachpark.com.tr*

Atlantis Waterpark, Marmaris

Swimming with Dolphins, Marmaris

At this dolphinarium on the coast near Marmaris, anyone over 12 can join the dolphins in the water for sessions of 5 or 10 minutes (under-18s must be accompanied by an adult). Under-12s are not permitted to swim with the dolphins, but the

Camel-riding on Side beach

centre offers a special programme that introduces younger children to these extraordinary creatures at the poolside. ◈ *Mares Hotel Coast 48700 • Map C4 • (0252) 455 24 33 • Adm • www.swim.withdolphins.com*

Swimming with dolphins

Explore Saklıkent Gorge

Tremendous fun for the whole family, a trip into the depths of Saklıkent Gorge involves splashing through ice-cold streams, scrambling over slippery rocks and getting plastered in mud wherever possible. Water shoes are essential and care should be taken when negotiating the larger rocks *(see p80)*.

Chimaera

Well worth staying up for, the Chimaera is best visited after dark, when the flickering flames that issue mysteriously from the rocky hillside above the village of Çirali provide a mesmerizing spectacle – as well as proving useful for passing hikers to brew their tea. A natural phenomenon caused by gas escaping from deep underground, the flames are reached by a short stretch of unlit path, for which a torch is essential *(see p88)*.

Camel-Riding, Side

A short ride on a camel lumbering along the eastern stretch of Side beach *(see p23)* or through some of the site's ancient ruins *(see p98)* will be a novel experience for most kids. These desert creatures are safe, slow and always led by a guide; but younger children should nonetheless be accompanied by an adult. ◈ *Map K5*

Kayaking to Kekova, Kaş

Several agencies in Kaş organize kayaking day trips to the sunken ruins at Kekova. Kayakers are towed by motor boats for much of the distance before being released to paddle about the region. Children sharing a kayak with a parent must be at least seven years old. ◈ *Map F6 • www.dragoman-turkey.com*

Left **Alize, Sarıgerme** Right **Kaya Wine House, Kaya Köyü**

🔟 Restaurants

1 Alize, Sarıgerme
Part of the Hilton golf and spa complex, this stylish restaurant with lovely sea views opens in the evenings with a select menu of Mediterranean dishes prepared by its team of award-winning chefs *(see p73)*.

2 Kaya Wine House, Kaya Köyü
This charming restaurant, whose covered wooden terrace offers views of the so-called "ghost town" *(see p80)*, is set in a carefully restored 400-year-old building with a fascinating history; before being abandoned in 1922, it was used as both a chapel and a jail *(see p85)*.

3 Coast@Gironda, Kalkan
This stylish restaurant with wonderful sea views offers traditional Turkish cuisine such as *Imam bayildi* (stuffed aubergine) as well as modern dishes that fuse Turkish with Thai and European elements *(see p85)*.

4 Divan Antalya Teras Restaurant, Antalya
Situated in the 5-star Divan Antalya Hotel that perches on a cliff-edge just beyond the city centre, the Teras shares the hotel's signature minimalism. Diners can enjoy sumptuous Mediterranean and Turkish cuisine on a broad terrace with stunning sea views *(see p92)*.

5 Hana Beach, Marmaris
One of the few restaurants in Marmaris to offer an escape from the relentless bustle of tourism, Hana Beach extends from the Elegance Hotel onto a wooden pier which separates diners from the nearby crowds. Low lighting, live jazz musicians, excellent international cuisine and great service combine to make for a memorable dining experience *(see p72)*.

6 Şelale Restaurant, Ulupınar
Every fish restaurant in town follows the trend of seating diners on platforms over the shallow River Ulupınar, but Şelale takes the theme one step further by positioning its many tables on a hillside above the cascading river. Specialities include baked trout and barbecued meat *(see p93)*.

Şelale Restaurant, Ulupınar

7 Chez Evy, Kaş

Run by a characterful French ex-pat, Chez Evy is the coast's most authentic rustic French restaurant. Portions are generous and there's a delightful garden for *plein air* dining *(see p85)*.

8 Tuti Restaurant, Bodrum

From its hilltop terrace above Bodrum, Tuti has unrivalled views of the town and the Aegean. Part of the Marmara Hotel, it offers enticing lunch and dinner menus that include some good fresh fish options as well as Turkish ravioli and salmon with avocado and ginger sauce *(see p92)*.

Moonlight, Side

9 Moonlight, Side

Perfect for fish-lovers (a wide variety of fresh fish is delivered daily by local fishermen), this outdoor, seaside restaurant is particularly attractive to holidaying couples in search of a romantic dinner *(see p103)*.

10 Lotis, Göcek

Popular with visiting yachters, this smart central restaurant with an international menu has a roof terrace from where diners can observe the busy marina. Service is brisk and efficient *(see p73)*.

Turkish Dishes

1 Köfte

Made from minced meat, parsley, egg and breadcrumbs, these simple yet delicious meatballs are often garnished with onions and hot chillies.

2 İskembe Çorbası

This popular dish – a kind of tripe soup – is found throughout the territories of the former Ottoman Empire.

3 Meze

Meze is a wide selection of small hot and cold dishes served as appetizers.

4 Guveç

This spicy meat-and-vegetable stew is slow-cooked in a closed ceramic pot to bring out the flavours.

5 Kebabs

There are many variants on the kebab. The most common is served in pita bread with salad and sauce.

6 Dolma

Vine leaves or cabbage leaves stuffed with meat or rice. Also known as *sarma*.

7 Musakka

Musakka is a typical Balkan dish of minced meat baked with aubergines, tomatoes and peppers.

8 İmam Bayıldı

This strangely named dish – literally, "the Imam fainted" – is a Turkish classic featuring aubergine stuffed with tomatoes and onions.

9 Fish

Popular throughout Turkey, fish is served poached, baked, fried and grilled.

10 Baklava

Thin layers of pastry are brushed with butter and filled with crushed pistachio nuts before being baked, then drowned in syrup – irresistible.

Left **Aphrodisias Museum** Centre **Side Roman Baths Museum** Right **Alanya Museum**

🔟 Museums

1 Ephesus Museum
Best appreciated after a trip to Ephesus *(see pp14–15)*, the museum's well-presented collection includes two stunning marble statues of the goddess Artemis and a recreation of a room in a Roman house. The museum is located in Selçuk, a short drive from Ephesus *(see pp16–17)*.

2 Bodrum Museum of Underwater Archaeology
This remarkable museum fills the halls of St Peter's Castle, built in the 15th century by the Knights Hospitaller. Dedicated to underwater archaeological finds in the region, the museum has a large collection of amphorae, glass and anchors collected from ancient shipwrecks. Replicas of two wrecks are on display. ⊗ *Map A4 • (0252) 316 25 16 • Open 9am–7pm Tue–Sun • Adm • www.bodrum-museum.com*

3 Marmaris Castle and Museum
Marmaris' 16th-century castle sits on a low hill above the harbour and what little remains of the old town. Damaged during World War I by a French destroyer, it was restored in the 1980s, and its crenellated walls now protect the town's museum. Archaeological finds are on display beside examples of traditional Turkish costume and carpets *(see p26)*.

Marmaris Castle and Museum

4 Aphrodisias Museum
The walls of this museum are lined with busts of governors, philosophers and military leaders, many originating from Aphrodisias' acclaimed school of sculpture. There is also a bronze of Kenan Erim, who led the site's excavation from 1961 until his death in 1990. ⊗ *Geyre Köyü, Karacasu, Aydın • Map B2 • (0256) 448 80 03 • Open 9am–5pm Tue–Sun (to 7pm in summer)*

5 Fethiye Museum
The archaeological wing of this smart museum has gold jewellery found at Tlos and Kaunos, as well as coins, grave steles and some well-preserved pottery and figurines. The ethnographic wing has a neatly arranged display of artifacts dating back to the Bronze Age. The courtyard is packed with statues, tombs and sarcophagi *(see pp28, 29)*.

Promissory stele in Fethiye Museum

6 Hierapolis Archaeological Museum

An intriguing array of finds from Hierapolis is on display in the restored Southern Baths. Exhibits include statuary discovered during the excavation of the theatre and a flawless child's sarcophagus with exquisitely detailed marble decoration *(see pp18, 19)*.

7 Antalya Archaeological Museum

Second only to the museums at Istanbul and Ankara in size and significance, Antalya's Archaeological Museum has an extensive collection gathered from nearby sites including Termessos, Perge, Side and Aspendos. The exhibits, displayed chronologically, date back to the Stone Age. Highlights include the Gallery of the Gods and the Hall of Sarcophagi *(see pp10–11)*.

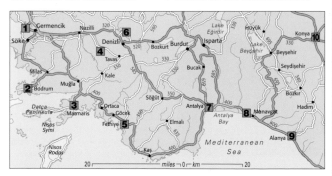

Sculpture of Hadrian, Antalya Archaeological Museum

8 Side Roman Baths Museum

The museum's small but fascinating collection fills the domed chambers of Side's restored 5th-century Roman baths. Among the exhibits are monuments inscribed in the ancient Sidetan language. Outside is a shaded courtyard filled with statuary and sarcophagi *(see pp22, 23)*.

9 Alanya Museum of Archaeology

Alanya's well-arranged museum has an impressive array of marble statues and sarcophagi collected from ancient sites in the region. One room has a reproduction of an Ottoman-era house furnished with antique rugs, ornaments and utensils. In the courtyard are more sarcophagi and a family of peacocks *(see pp24, 25)*.

10 Mevlâna Museum, Konya

Regarded as one of the world's greatest mystics, Mevlâna – better known in the West as the poet Rumi – founded the Sufi brotherhood of whirling dervishes in the 13th century, in Konya. His mausoleum and the original dervish lodge became a museum in 1926. Visitors can view Mevlâna's elaborately decorated tomb and various related exhibits. ◈ Selimiye Cad, Mevlâna Mah • Map M2 • (0332) 351 12 15 • Open 9am–5pm daily • Adm • Women should cover their head and shoulders

Left **Saklıkent Gorge** Right **Eğirdir lake**

Escapes from the Heat

1 Lycian Way
While much of the Lycian Way tracks the coastline, several sections take hikers to higher – and cooler – ground. The 26-km (16-mile) route from Gökçeören to Kaş rises to around 900 m (2,953 ft) before descending to the sea; the difficult 27-km (17-mile) section from Zeytin to Finike reaches 1,800 m (5,906 ft); and the 52-km (33-mile) route from Çirali to Ovacik includes an ascent of Mount Olympos – not for faint hearts *(see pp20–21)*.

2 Ulupınar
There's no better way to cool down than to eat out with your feet in an icy stream. Ulupınar's fish restaurants feature tables on platforms perched above the shallow waters of the Ulupınar river and shaded by dense foliage. Fresh trout baked in a clay dish is one of their delicious specialities *(see p90)*.

Outdoor tables at Ulupınar

3 Muğla
This pleasant provincial town lies some 30 km (19 miles) inland. It sits beneath craggy hills at an altitude of around 650 m (2,133 ft), ensuring a refreshing break from the oppressive summer heat of the coast. Many of the old town's Ottoman-era houses have been restored, and there's an absorbing museum, as well as two historic mosques and a working *hamam* dating back to 1258 *(see p110)*.

4 Eğirdir Lake
Eğirdir lake's tree-shaded shores and cool summer evenings attract a mixture of picnicking locals and tourists in search of a peaceful break. Part of Turkey's appealing lake district, Eğirdir is the country's fourth-largest lake, with an area of 482 km sq (186 sq miles). On its southwest shore is the town of Eğirdir. Both town and lake were formerly known as Eğridir, from the original Greek name Akrotiri. Unfortunately, Eğridir means "crooked" in Turkish, so in the 1980s it was changed to Eğirdir ("she is spinning") to remove the negative association *(see p109)*.

5 Tahtalı Teleferik Cable Car
A trip to the summit of Mount Olympos using one of the longest cable-car systems in the world is a great way to cool down, and takes just 10 minutes. Passengers can dine at the mountain-top restaurant, with stunning panoramic views *(see p109)*.

Tahtalı Teleferik cable car

Caves

6 Descending into dark, subterranean caverns where temperatures hover around 18°C (64°F) is another good way to beat the heat. Damlataş Cave *(see p98)* and Dim Cave *(see p99)* are full of stalactites and stalagmites. Karain Cave *(see 90)* has a fascinating history; it was inhabited by humans as long ago as the Paleolithic era.

Saklıkent Gorge

7 This deep, narrow limestone gorge remains cool throughout the day, and the water that gushes out from its cavities is stunningly cold. Simple water shoes (which can be purchased at nearby kiosks) are essential for walking into the gorge over slippery rocks *(see p80)*.

Rafting at Köprülü Canyon

8 You're guaranteed a soaking at Turkey's top rafting spot. The relatively tame rapids are suitable for beginners. Rafting groups are kitted out with wetsuits, buoyancy aids and helmets. Trips can be arranged by agents at Alanya and Antalya *(see p97)*.

Turkish Baths

9 It's hardly a way to escape the heat, but it's certainly a different way to enjoy it. Turks have had a *hamam* culture since Roman times, and some of the baths are several hundred years old. In touristy areas they are often mixed-sex, while smaller local baths have different hours for men and women.

Bird-Watching

10 Two major bird migration routes pass over Turkey in spring and autumn, and the country itself is home to an enormous variety of birds. One of the best coastal birding spots lies around the Dalyan river and Köyceğiz lake *(see p69)*. Belek is also known for its birdlife, and Eğirdir lake is home to water birds, including the pygmy cormorant and tufted duck. ⏺ *www.birdwatch turkey.com • www.dalyanbirding.com*

Rafting at Köprülü Canyon

Left **James Dean Bar, Alanya** Centre **Beach Club, Marmaris** Right **Greenhouse, Marmaris**

🔟 Nightlife Spots

1 Halikarnas, Bodrum
This seafront club is jam-packed throughout the summer, with spectacular dance shows backed by deafening music and dazzling lighting. There are drinks promotions most evenings. Foam cannons turn Friday and Saturday nights into very messy occasions. 🕲 *Cumhuriyet Cad 178 • Map A4 • Adm*

2 Beach Club, Marmaris
One of the loudest and busiest clubs in Marmaris, Beach Club's vast outdoor dance floor is entered through the unassuming doors of an old house on Bar Street. Ministry of Sound DJs play guest slots in high season to an ecstatic crowd *(see p74)*.

3 Greenhouse, Marmaris
One of the first small clubs to move into Bar Street back in 1988, Greenhouse has evolved into a massive open-air venue with a sound system powerful enough to drown out neighbouring clubs. Attractions include transvestite dancers and weekly sets from international DJs *(see p74)*.

Club Ally, Antalya

4 Deep Blue Bar, Fethiye
Fethiye's Bar Street is lined with quirky clubs and bars squeezed into the old houses of Paspatur. A great place to relax and enjoy a cocktail, Deep Blue Bar is renowned for its friendly vibe and live local bands playing anything from blues to rock or jazz. 🕲 *Hamam Sok, Paspatur • Map E5*

5 Robin Hood, Alanya
At the heart of Alanya's noisy nightlife quarter, Robin Hood occupies a large detached building with DJs playing different styles on each of its four floors. The rooftop terrace affords excellent views of the harbour and the surrounding mayhem *(see p101)*.

6 James Dean Bar, Alanya
Turkish male dancers gyrate enticingly on podiums flanking the entrance to this loud Alanya nightspot where DJs play the latest Western pop hits at full volume. The two open-air dance-floors are rammed with partygoers throughout the summer. Plastic palm trees and Roman columns provide the decor *(see p101)*.

7 Club Ally, Antalya
One of Antalya's swankiest clubs, Ally occupies a prime position beside the old city walls. It's an outdoor venue where the party people perch on high stools beneath a mass of hi-tech lights and speakers that pump out pop and dance tunes. Advance reservation recommended *(see p91)*.

Club Arma, Antalya

Club Arma, Antalya

This chic club and restaurant has an open-air dance floor beside the harbour where tireless podium dancers provide entertainment for a well-dressed and rather static crowd. There's no entrance fee, but the drink prices make up for it *(see p91)*.

Bar Street, Kuşadası

The Kuşadası version of Marmaris's Bar Street is somewhat less atmospheric than its southerly counterpart, as it's in a district of modern buildings with smaller bars; but if bucket cocktails, deafening music and party games are what you're here for, then there's plenty of fun to be had. ◈ *Barlar Sok • Map A2*

Kadir's Treehouse Club, Olympos

A refreshing alternative to the crowded clubs at larger resorts, the outdoor Treehouse Club is built from rickety logs and has a bonfire for clubbers to dance around. The DJ's CD collection inclines to the Golden Oldies, but the merry crowd of Turkish and international backpackers hardly seems to care *(see p91)*.

Top 10 Turkish Drinks

Tea
Turkey's most popular drink is served black and sweet in small tulip-shaped glasses. An offer of tea is considered a sign of friendship and hospitality.

Coffee
Strong and sweet, Turkish coffee is made by mixing ground coffee with sugar and boiling it in a special pot.

Ayran
Particularly effective as an antidote to the summer heat, this refreshing drink is made from yogurt mixed with water and a little salt.

Rakı
This strong, aniseed-flavoured spirit is commonly served with mezes *(see p53)*.

Beer
Increasingly popular with Turks, good-quality beer is brewed in Turkey by Efes and Tuborg. International brands are also available.

Wine
Turkey has a number of reputable wineries. Kavaklidere produces particularly good Anatolian wines.

Fresh Orange Juice
Stalls on street corners and beachfronts everywhere sell freshly squeezed orange juice.

Sahlep
Sahlep is a winter drink made from hot milk and mixed with a flour ground from dried orchid tubers.

Boza
This thick, sour drink made from fermented wheat and often used as a hangover cure is definitely an acquired taste.

Şira
Sweet and non-alcoholic, *şira* is made from fermented grape juice.

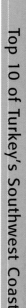

Left **Shops in Paspatur, Fethiye** Centre **Bodrum Carpets** Right **Grand Bazaar, Marmaris**

Shops and Markets

Kaleiçi Bazaar, Antalya

Antalya's Kaleiçi Bazaar is concentrated around Uzun Çarşı Sokak, a paved street of restored Ottoman-era houses that slopes down towards the harbour. Carpets, leather goods, backgammon boards, baklava and Turkish Delight are among the many items on sale *(see pp8–9)*.

Old Town, Kaş

Kaş's carefree charm has attracted artists and artisans for decades. The narrow, cobbled streets of the old town are now home to many of their small shops and studios, where visitors can find handmade jewellery, furniture, clothing and artwork *(see pp30–31)*.

Paspatur, Fethiye

Fethiye's old-town shopping quarter, known as Paspatur, is a lively area of brightly painted bars, restaurants and shops set in atmospheric buildings hung with ivy and flowers. The shops sell the usual touristy goods as well as some lovely artworks and fine handmade crafts *(see p28)*.

Grand Bazaar, Marmaris

Although far less grand than its Istanbul namesake, this bazaar is certainly well-stocked. Hundreds of small shops bursting with everything from "quality fakes" to souvenirs and kitchenware shelter beneath the simple plastic roofing, with eager shopkeepers calling out "Where are you from?" to every passer-by *(see p27)*.

Side Bazaar

Side's bazaar is a pleasant pedestrianized quarter of touristy shops, *pensions* and restaurants housed in Ottoman-style buildings. Its central thoroughfare, Liman Caddesi, follows the same route as the old Roman town's main street, although there's no sign of that today *(see pp22–3)*.

Grand Bazaar, Kuşadası

The covered bazaar beside the harbour has a mixture of stalls and smart, glass-fronted shops. Colourful cushion-covers, carpets, bags and clothes clutter pavements and shop windows. Prices are rarely displayed, so be prepared to haggle *(see p112)*.

Netsel Marina, Marmaris

Situated within the marina, this small, secluded mall of high-end boutiques sells expensive designer clothes and accessories. It's something of a contrast to the bustle of the nearby bazaar, where fakes are flogged for a fraction of the price *(see p27)*.

Netsel Marina, Marmaris

Kalkan

Despite being a relatively small town, Kalkan has plenty of shops, offering a wide choice of goods, from arty souvenirs and handmade jewellery to carpets and designer clothes. Many of the shops can be found along the steep, narrow streets leading down to the harbour *(see p80)*.

View towards Kalkan harbour

Alanya Bazaar

Alanya's covered bazaar is filled with small shops selling a broad range of clothes, shoes and souvenirs. There are no fixed prices, so you'll have to haggle with shopkeepers whose starting price is usually double what they expect. For a more western shopping experience head for the town centre, which is jammed with modern shops *(see p25)*.

Bodrum Bazaar

Occupying the bewildering maze of the old town's narrow streets, the bazaar is a delight to explore. You'll find tailors and cobblers squeezed in alongside jewellers, galleries and carpet shops, all stacked to the ceiling with enticing goods. If you need a break, the whole area is laced with bars, cafés and kebab shops *(see p112)*.

Top 10 Things to Buy

1 Carpets
Sold in every bazaar, Turkey's colourful carpets come in an enormous variety of patterns and styles.

2 Ceramics
Intricately patterned and brightly coloured, most of the ceramics on sale originate from Kütahaya in western Turkey.

3 Meerschaum
This surprisingly light white stone is carved with great precision to produce items like pipes and chess pieces.

4 Textiles
Turkey is a renowned textile producer and a great place to pick up inexpensive cotton and silk items.

5 Leather Goods
Bags, jackets, belts and trousers come in all manner of styles, usually copied from big-name designers.

6 Copperware
The ancient art of copper-smithing is still practised in some areas – typical souvenirs are kettles and engraved plates.

7 Local Delicacies
Turkish delight is everywhere, and makes a great gift to take back home. Halva, nuts and spices are also in plentiful supply.

8 Jewellery
Numerous shops sell attractive silver and gold jewellery. For unusual designs, try galleries and craft shops.

9 Nazar Boncuğu
These blue-and-white amulets come in all sizes and are supposed to protect wearers from the "evil eye".

10 Nargiles
Still used in Turkish cafés, decorative water pipes make interesting souvenirs.

Left **Gloria Golf Club, Belek** Right **Rafting at Köprülü Canyon**

Sporting Activities

Golf
1 With its 14 international-standard courses, Belek remains the top Turkish destination for golfers. Spread along the coast from Kumköy to Karadayı, the superb courses – designed by some of the world's best players – offer year-round golfing.

Scuba Diving
2 The coastal waters provide excellent diving conditions from April to November, with visibility of up to 30 m (98 ft). Most resorts have well-established diving schools offering everything from trial dives to full PADI courses. Divers can visit wrecks, reefs, underwater caves and canyons.
◈ www.divingturkey.com

Water Sports
3 All the major resorts offer the usual range of water sports, such as water-skiing and parasailing, as well as some wild and wacky ones – like being pulled at high speed on a rubber "banana" or chair. Jet-skiing is also common, but is often banned at smaller beaches to avoid disturbance.

Rafting and Kayaking
4 Köprülü Canyon *(see p97)* is by far the best spot for rafting. Numerous companies offer trips through its 14 km (9 miles) of narrow gorges. The leisurely alternative is to raft down the gently flowing river from Saklıkent Gorge. A popular kayaking daytrip is from Kaş to the sunken ruins of Kekova *(see p21)*.

Wind- and Kite-Surfing
5 The best wind- and kite-surfing beaches can be found along the western Aegean coast, where warm winds provide perfect conditions. There are reliable centres on the Bodrum Peninsula and at Alaçati on the Çesme Peninsula, west of İzmir. Köyceğiz lake also has favourable conditions for windsurfing. ◈ www.fenerwindsurf.com • www.alacati.com

Hiking
6 The Lycian Way is the only well-marked trail in the region *(see pp20–21)*. It covers both mountainous and coastal terrain and includes an ascent of Mount Olympos. Guided walks in the mountains around Eğirdir lake *(see p109)* can be arranged by the Eğirdir Outdoor Centre, whose owner also runs the Eğirdir Lale Hostel nearby.
◈ *Eğirdir Outdoor Centre: Opposite the harbour at the start of the causeway • Map J2 • (0542) 241 72 13 (mob)*

Water sports centre on Adrasan Beach, near Kemer

7 Mountain Biking

While some of the larger hotels offer bikes for local use, those in search of more adventurous riding can join organized tours with companies such as Kaunos Tours in Dalyan or the Eğirdir Outdoor Centre, which rents out good-quality bikes and provides maps and route advice. ⊗ www.kaunostours.com

8 Sailing

Sailing enthusiasts can choose anything from single-cabin self-sail yachts and catamarans to fully crewed *gulets* accommodating up to 32 people. Smart marinas dotted along the coast provide first-rate facilities. Tour companies include Budget Sailing at Göçek and UK-based Nautilus Yachting. ⊗ www.budgetsailing.com • www.nautilus-yachting.com

9 Surfing

Surfing is far less popular in Turkey than other water sports, but Patara (see p80) and İztuzu (see p70) beaches usually have good waves. Simple bodyboards can be found at most beach shops, but serious surfers will need to bring their own boards.

10 Skiing

The closest ski resort to the coast, 26 km (16 miles) from the city of Isparta, is at Mount Davraz, which offers skiers lovely views of Eğirdir lake far below. Small but increasingly popular, the resort has around 6 km (4 miles) of intermediate and advanced ski runs, as well as several nursery slopes. Accommodation is in the Sirene Davraz Ski and Wellness Hotel, which has two restaurants serving Turkish and international cuisine. The season begins on 1 December. ⊗ Map H3 • (0246) 267 20 28 • www.davraz.com.tr

Top 10 Diving Spots

1 Kaş

Kaş (see pp30–31) is a popular destination, with around 16 diving centres. ⊗ www.sundiving.com

2 Kemer

Kemer has a number of reputable centres. ⊗ Map H5 • www.octopus-kemer.com

3 Ölüdeniz

There are several wrecks close to Ölüdeniz (see p79). ⊗ www.blueworlddiving.com

4 Bodrum

Dive sites near Bodrum (see p106) include Bubble Cave, entered through a narrow hole. ⊗ www.happybubbles.com

5 Fethiye

Fethiye (see pp28–9) has several dive centres offering trial dives and professional diving instructor courses. ⊗ www.elitedivingcentre.com

6 Adrasan

Adrasan (see p87) is close to caves, canyons and wrecks. ⊗ www.diving-adrasan.com

7 Antalya

Sunk by a torpedo in 1941, the wreck of the supply ship St Didier lies close to Antalya harbour (see pp8–9). ⊗ www.yunusdiving.com

8 Sarıgerme

This small beach resort (see p70) has a couple of dive centres offering courses and trips. ⊗ www.sarigerme.net

9 Olympos

There are at least 20 different diving spots in the vicinity of Olympos (see p87). ⊗ www.olymposdiving.com

10 Kalkan

A wrecked steamship, underwater walls, reefs and canyons can be found near Kalkan (see p80). ⊗ www.dolphinscubateam.com

Jeep Safari near Kaş

🔟 Adventurous Activities

1 Canyoning
This exciting combination of abseiling, climbing, swimming, walking and scrambling through narrow gorges and up and down steep rock faces and waterfalls requires a very good head for heights, a wetsuit and climbing shoes. The best place to try it with a qualified guide is Saklıkent Gorge (see p80). ☎ (252) 659 00 74
• www.saklikentgorge.com

Saklıkent Gorge

2 Bungee-Jumping
In this relatively new addition to Turkey's portfolio of adventurous activities, mobile cranes at Alanya (see pp24–5) and Ölüdeniz (see p79) now offer bungee-jumping from a cage lifted to a height of 40 m (131 ft). Jumpers receive full instructions from qualified trainers.

3 Rock Climbing
One of the largest climbing walls in the southwest region is at Geyikbayırı, 25 km (16 miles) from Antalya, with more than 500 routes from 25–60 m (82–197 ft). Ranging from easy to very difficult, they include overhangs and a route known as the "Aquaduct" – considered Turkey's hardest. Climbers without their own gear can join organized climbing trips from Olympos (see p87). ☎ (242) 892 13 16 • www.olymposrockclimbing.com

4 Jeep Safaris
These bone-shaking trips over rocky tracks, through rivers and up ludicrously steep hills are great fun and hugely popular with tourists. Most resorts offer all-inclusive day trips in modern 4WD vehicles that can seat up to 12 passengers. Swimming stops are usually factored in, along with lunch breaks at traditional restaurants. ☎ (242) 312 80 66 • www.safariturkey.com

5 Quad Bikes
These chunky machines offer a great way to get off the beaten track and can be hired individually or in a group. Ölüdeniz (see p79) and Bodrum (see p108) are both well known for organized tours. Brakes should be checked before setting out. Novices should choose low-power bikes. ☎ (242) 753 61 00 • www.vigotour.com

6 Paintball
Of the few paintball outfits along the coast, the most reliable is Çamlica at Çetibeli, between Marmaris and Muğla. Combatants are provided with camouflaged overalls and full face masks for battles that take place in forested terrain littered with a variety of obstacles. The centre also arranges quad bike tours. ☎ Çamlica, Çetibeli Mevkii • Map C4 • (252) 426 01 66

Some of these activities – such as coasteering – carry a degree of risk. Be sure to take out insurance when you book.

7 Paragliding

Ölüdeniz is Turkey's top paragliding centre, with over 50,000 flights a season. Gliders launch from Babadağ Mountain at 1,980 m (6,496 ft) and take around 40 minutes to reach the beach. Tandem flights with a qualified instructor require no previous experience. ◈ *Hector Paragliding: (252) 617 07 05; www.hectorparagliding.com • Dolce Vita Travel: (242) 836 16 10; www.dolcevitatravel.org*

8 Horse Trekking

Despite the suitable terrain, there are few riding centres in the region. Based in Ölüdeniz, Activities Unlimited organizes daily rides to the abandoned village of Kaya Köyü and back. Just outside Kemer, Berke Ranch offers trekking in the nearby mountains. ◈ *Activities Unlimited: (252) 616 63 16; www.activities-unlimited-turkey.com • Berke Ranch: (242) 818 03 33; www.hotelberkeranch.com*

Paragliding at Ölüdeniz

Horse trekking near Kemer

9 Microlight Flights

Fly-South operates a pair of two-seater microlights from Hisarönü, just outside Fethiye *(see p79)*. They run daily trips throughout the summer and the microlights can remain airborne for up to four hours. Popular flights are to Patara Beach for a swim and to Kalkan for lunch. You can also take the easy option and fly over Babadağ Mountain. ◈ *Map E5 • www.fly-south.org*

10 Coasteering

A relatively new activity and definitely not for the faint-hearted, coasteering – also known as coastal traversing – involves climbing along, rather than up, a coastal rock face, above deep water and without ropes. Coasteerers are equipped with helmets, wetsuits and buoyancy aids, and the idea is to swim where it isn't possible to climb. The only agency currently offering coasteering is Dragoman in Kaş *(see p118)*.

AROUND TURKEY'S SOUTHWEST COAST

TOP 10 OF TURKEY'S SOUTHWEST COAST

Left **Marmaris' old town** Right **Datça's harbour**

East from Marmaris

Many of the tiny bays and idyllic beaches along this rugged coastline are inaccessible by car, but ideal for the yachts and day boats that cruise the region using Marmaris and Göcek as their bases. Land-lovers are not without options – there are great beaches at Sarıgerme, Turunç and Dalyan, and the Datça Peninsula has a number of lovely bays that can be reached by road. For entertainment, Marmaris is second to none for high-energy nightlife, while Dalyan has a far smaller and more laid-back bar scene. Dalyan is also the starting point for river-boat tours to the ruins of Kaunos and the vast Lake Köyceğiz, where tourists can wallow in the famous mud baths.

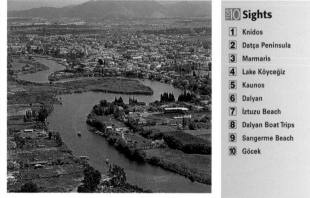

The resort town of Dalyan, by the tranquil Dalyan river

🔟 Sights

1. Knidos
2. Datça Peninsula
3. Marmaris
4. Lake Köyceğiz
5. Kaunos
6. Dalyan
7. İztuzu Beach
8. Dalyan Boat Trips
9. Sarıgerme Beach
10. Göcek

Preceding pages **Boats in the fishing harbour at Kuşadası**

The ancient city of Knidos, on the Datça Peninsula

Knidos

Once a powerful Greek settlement that straddled the Mediterranean and Aegean Seas, Knidos was founded in the 4th century BC. It was famous throughout the ancient world for its nude statue of the goddess Aphrodite, which drew worshippers from miles around. The statue has not survived, but the circular foundations of the open-air temple in which it was installed lie high on the hillside. Although the site has yet to be fully excavated, the well-preserved theatre and mosaic floors of a Byzantine basilica suggest that much more remains to be discovered. ◈ *Map A5 • Open 8am–7pm daily • Adm*

Datça Peninsula

In places, this narrow spit of land between the Mediterranean and Aegean seas is just 800 m (875 yds) wide. During ancient times it was home to a population of 70,000 people who settled around Knidos and profited handsomely from the activity of the busy trading port. Nowadays the area is more familiar as a quiet retreat from the busier coastal resorts. Using the pleasant town of Datça as a base, tourists can explore some of the many secluded bays by boat or car, and visit the ruins of Knidos at the peninsula's western tip. ◈ *Map B5*

Marmaris

Since the 1980s, Marmaris has grown from a sleepy fishing village into a bustling tourist resort; but what it may nowadays lack in character and atmosphere, it makes up for through sheer volume of tourist facilities. Countless tour boats line the harbour, a vast purpose-built grand bazaar offers innumerable shopping opportunities, the infamous Bar Street *(see p74)* provides some of the coast's best nightlife and both the harbour and the town's Long Beach are jammed with seafront restaurants. For those in search of period ambience, the castle and the old town provide a taste of the past *(see pp26–7)*.

Lake Köyceğiz

Köyceğiz – Turkish for "Water Heaven" – covers 6,300 hectares (24 sq miles). To the south it fragments into a maze of channels, split by reed beds, that flow to the sea via the Dalyan Strait. Home to all manner of wildlife including huge catfish that attract keen fishermen, it's also a well-trodden spot for windsurfing and sailing. The famous mud and thermal baths on its shore *(see p50)* are a popular stop-off for tour boats. ◈ *Map D4*

Lake Köyceğiz

Kaunos

Said to have been founded by Kaunos, son of the Lycian King Miletus and grandson of the god Apollo, the port of Kaunos thrived for centuries under a succession of dynasties until its harbour silted up in the Middle Ages. The remains are

Temple remains at Kaunos, near Dalyan

best accessed by boat from Dalyan *(see below)*; most impressive are the theatre, acropolis, temple and tombs. Work on the large half-finished tomb cut into the cliff face is thought to have been abandoned after the town fell to Alexander the Great in 334 BC. ✎ *Map D5*

Dalyan

The main departure point for boat trips up and down the Dalyan Strait, this small town has developed into a pleasant tourist resort. Restaurants and bars have taken full advantage of its idyllic location, setting up laid-back riverside hangouts with shaded gardens and views of the dramatic Lycian rock tombs in the cliffs opposite. The name Dalyan – "fish traps" – derives from the fishing of bass, mullet and sea bream that has gone on here since ancient times. ✎ *Map D5*

Endangered Loggerhead Turtles

Reaching lengths of up to 2 m (6.5 ft) and weighing as much as 150 kg (331 lbs), loggerheads *(Caretta caretta)* are the world's largest turtles. Sadly, the destruction of their nesting sites at beaches around the world has threatened their survival. Turkey's main nesting beaches at İztuzu, Patara, and Çıralı are strictly protected from development.

İztuzu Beach

This glorious expanse of sand, stretching for 5 km (3 miles) across the mouth of the Dalyan Strait, is one of Turkey's best beaches. Also known as Turtle Beach, it's the nesting ground for endangered loggerhead sea turtles. The beach attracted international attention in 1986 when British naturalist David Bellamy became involved in a successful campaign to protect it from developers. Today the golden sands and crystal-clear waters remain completely unspoiled; even the few beach bars are camouflaged with dry reeds. ✎ *Map D5*

İztuzu beach with freshwater lagoon behind

Dalyan Boat Trips

Dalyan is noted for the small boats that chug along its river, taking passengers upstream to Lake Köyceğiz, with its popular mud and thermal baths, and downstream to the ruins at Kaunos and on through the Dalyan delta to İztuzu beach. Boat captains will do their best to arrange sightings of loggerhead turtles. The varied habitats of lake, river, delta and beach provide first-rate opportunities for bird-watching. Visitors to the lake can stop off at Hapishane Adası, a small 19th-century prison island. ✎ *Map D5*

9 Sarıgerme Beach

This marvellous beach was subjected to excessive development in the 1980s but has been tidied up in recent years. A park-and-ride system operates for cars, with a regular shuttle running between the beach and the car park, some distance away. Visitors are charged a small entrance fee, which goes towards the cost of keeping the 7-km (4-mile) beach up to the standards of the many 5-star resorts that nestle within the surrounding woods. Jet-skis are banned, but this is a great spot for kite- and wind-surfing.
⊗ Map D5 • Adm

10 Göcek

Set in a secluded bay, the town's natural harbour has been utilized since Lycian times, but there are few historic remains in the vicinity. Of greater interest to today's visitors are the six marinas which have been built over the past couple of decades to accommodate the increasing number of yachts and tour boats using the harbour. The town itself has been declared an area of special protection, and this has kept development to a minimum – there are very few large hotels and the nightlife is low-key. ⊗ Map D5

Yachts moored in Göcek's harbour

Marmaris in a Day

Morning

Start at the Atatürk statue on the seafront, a popular meeting-point for locals. Then follow the harbour until you reach the **Tourist Information Centre** (see p26), which provides useful maps. Enter the narrow streets of the **Old Town** to the left of the tourist office and follow signs for "Kale/Castle" up to **Marmaris Castle and Museum** (see p54). There are lovely views from the castle towers. Wander back down into the Old Town, where you can either spend the rest of the morning exploring the **Grand Bazaar**, or head for the **Bazaar Hamam** (see p27) opposite the Old Mosque to enjoy an invigorating steam bath. A right turn outside the bathhouse leads to **Netsel Marina** (see p42) for yet more shopping opportunities and lunch at the **Pineapple Restaurant** (see p72) facing the marina.

Afternoon

Walk along the seafront past the moored yachts to your left. Beyond the tourist office, the private yachts are replaced by a long line of *gulets* offering boat trips of varying length. Join a cruise to Paradise Island and Phosphorous Cave, or simply slump into a lounger on **Long Beach** (see p27) and spend the afternoon by the sea. There's an incredible choice of evening entertainment. Choose from any of the restaurants facing Long Beach; **Hana Beach** (see p72) is the calmest but many others offer live entertainment. After dinner, you can join the throngs of partygoers as they head towards **Bar Street** (Old Town) (see p74).

Left **Ristorante Fellini** Centre **Pineapple** Right **Aysha**

Restaurants in Marmaris

1 Hana Beach
Set on a wooden pier, this sophisticated restaurant offers an excellent menu and faultless service. Live jazz and subdued lighting enhance the experience. ◈ *Elegance Hotel, Siteler Mah 209, Sok 4 • Map C4 • (0252) 417 78 78 • €€€€€*

2 Ristorante Fellini
One of many restaurants with large harbourside terraces, Fellini occupies an old stone house beneath the castle. The menu is international. ◈ *Barbaros Cad 61 • Map P5 • (0252) 413 08 26 • €€€€*

3 Pineapple
Enjoy delightful dishes like Anatolian lamb and chicken-and-coconut curry on a lovely shaded terrace just a stone's throw from hundreds of moored yachts. ◈ *Netsel Marina • Map Q5 • (0252) 412 09 76 • Open year-round • €€€*

4 Taj Mahal
Predictably popular with Brits craving a taste of home, the Taj Mahal serves fish 'n' chips, as well as a range of familiar Indian dishes including various kormas and vindaloos. ◈ *Kemal Elgin Bulvari, Karacan Plaza 54/17 • Map C4 • (0252) 417 44 12 • €€€*

5 Antique
This lovely Italian restaurant within the marina is a great place to escape from the crowds and enjoy superb food in an intimate environment. ◈ *Netsel Marina • Map Q5 • (0252) 413 29 55 • €€€€€*

6 Portofino
Set back from the beach, the Portofino offers a slightly calmer alternative to its neighbours. Pizza and pasta form the bulk of the menu. ◈ *Uzunyali Cad 228, Sok 6/A • Map C4 • (0252) 413 22 61 • €€€*

7 Aysha
Set right in the middle of the busy beachfront promenade, this lively place offers both Turkish and international food. Sample shisha pipes while you watch the karaoke next door. ◈ *Uzunyali Cad 50 • Map C4 • (0252) 412 52 94 • €€€*

8 Faros
This busy beachfront eatery has a pleasant atmosphere, good-value menu and live music every night. For daytime users, there's a plentiful supply of loungers and beach umbrellas. ◈ *Uzunyali Cad 207, Sok 96 • Map C4 • (0252) 417 78 86 • €€€*

9 La Fleur
With comfy sofas facing the harbour, La Fleur is certainly an attractive proposition. On the menu are such delicious options as fresh fish, beef chili and onion steak. ◈ *Barbaros Cad 113 • Map P5 • (0252) 412 14 35 • €€€€*

10 Anfi
This well-established bar and restaurant catering almost exclusively to British tourists has everything from full English breakfast to Sky TV. ◈ *Anfitiyatro Karsisi • Map C4 • (0252) 413 30 24 • €€€*

Restaurants are open between early April and late October unless otherwise stated.

Price Categories

For a three-course meal for one with half a bottle of wine (or equivalent meal), taxes and extra charges.

€	under €15
€€	€15–€25
€€€	€25–€30
€€€€	€30–€35
€€€€€	over €35

Gölbaşi, Dalyan

TOP10 Regional Restaurants

1 Alize, Sarıgerme
One of the Hilton Dalaman's six exclusive restaurants, the superbly styled Alize features marble flooring, high ceilings and exquisite Mediterranean cuisine. ◈ *Hilton Dalaman Resort and Spa • Map D5 • (0252) 286 86 86 • €€€€€*

2 Lotis, Göcek
Beef Stroganoff and full English breakfast are on the menu at this smartly furnished restaurant. Excellent desserts. ◈ *Belediye Dükkanlari, Kordon Boyu A Blok 1 • Map D5 • (0252) 645 13 13 • €€€€*

3 Barbaros, Göcek
This pleasant, family-run restaurant right beside the harbour offers a good selection of Turkish cuisine including grilled meats, fresh fish and *musakka*. ◈ *İskele Meydanı Belediye Çarşısı • Map B5 • (0252) 645 30 56 • €€€*

4 Ogun's Place, Datça
Set in an idyllic location in the diminutive Hayit Buku Bay, Ogun's Place serves freshly baked bread and delicious dishes made from local produce. ◈ *Mesudiye Köyü Hayitbükü • Map B5 • (0252) 728 00 23 • €€€€*

5 Tuna Restaurant, Datça
Popular with Turkish tourists, this is a great place to sample typical local cuisine. Fresh fish is delivered daily; diners can choose from a refrigerated display. ◈ *İskele Mah, Kumluk Plaji Mevkii 16 • Map B5 • (0252) 712 38 79 • €€€*

6 Yesim, Datça
Expect faultless local dishes and friendly, efficient service at this wonderfully relaxed garden restaurant beside the beach, equipped with hammocks, bean bags and comfy chairs. ◈ *Kargi Koyu • Map B5 • (0252) 712 83 99 • €€€*

7 La Vie, Dalyan
La Vie offers good music and decent international cuisine. From its spacious, shaded terrace there are great views of the nearby cliff tombs. ◈ *Maras Mah, Saglik Sok 5 • Map D5 • (0252) 284 40 38 • €€€€*

8 Gölbaşı, Dalyan
This atmospheric riverside restaurant just outside of Dalyan can be reached by car or boat. Tables are set on wooden piers amidst tall reeds. ◈ *Iztuzu Yolu Üzeri 43 • Map D5 • (0252) 284 44 10 • €€€*

9 Ceyhan, Dalyan
This secluded restaurant occupies a charming riverside spot from which diners can watch the tour boats chugging by. The international menu features a particularly good choice of salads. ◈ *Gülpinar Mah, Sahil Kenari • Map D5 • (0252) 284 53 87 • €€€€*

10 Mutlu Kardeşler, Köyceğiz
This good-value eatery in the centre of town serves traditional Turkish dishes and *pide* – Turkish pizza. ◈ *Fevzipaşa Cad, Atapark Yani • Map D4 • (0252) 262 24 82 • Open year-round • €€*

Left **Greenhouse** Right **B-52**

Bars

Beach Club, Marmaris
Considered the town's top venue, Beach Club attracts the likes of Ministry of Sound, playing intense techno and pop to the crowds filling its cavernous interior. ◈ *Bar Street • Map Q5*

Greenhouse, Marmaris
Pumping out the latest dance tunes, Greenhouse's open-air arena features hi-tech lighting, drinks promotions and raised dance podiums manned by transvestite dancers and topless Turkish boys. ◈ *Bar Street • Map P5*

Crazy Daisy, Marmaris
With an immense sound system, frenetic light shows and frequent foam parties, Crazy Daisy has gained a reputation for wildness that keeps it packed with inebriated punters every night. ◈ *Bar Street • Map Q5*

Talk of the Town Cheers, Marmaris
This bustling place on Long Beach has palm-shaded beachfront tables. The huge bar runs regular drinks promotions and puts on a nightly cabaret show to keep the customers happy. ◈ *Uzunyali Cad (Long Beach) • Map C4*

B-52, Marmaris
A scaled-down alternative to the massive neighbouring clubs, B-52 is an atmospheric bar with bare-brick walls where musicians perform live rock and pop every night. ◈ *Bar Street • Map Q5*

Aquarium Bar, Marmaris
One of the town's oldest tourist bars, Aquarium faces the harbour and is a great place for huge "fishbowl" cocktails that can be shared by a whole table. ◈ *Barbaros Cad 51 • Map P6*

Barkas, Marmaris
A nightclub with a difference, Barkas is a converted three-floor ferry which sails twice nightly around the bay (11:30pm–3:30am and 4–7:30am). Water shuttles return exhausted partygoers to the shore throughout the night. ◈ *Marmaris Harbour • Map P6 • Adm*

Jazz Bar, Dalyan
The Jazz Bar is a wonderfully laid-back place with log tables and quirky furnishings. The house band plays live blues and jazz to a lively mixture of tourists and locals till late. ◈ *Gulpinar Mah 30 • Map D5*

Sun Ray Lounge, Dalyan
At this chilled-out Dalyan bar, bean bags and shisha pipes provide relaxation in the riverside garden while live bands play rock, pop, blues and Turkish tunes. The staff are friendly and polite. ◈ *Maraş Cad • Map D5*

Fun Pub, Dalyan
Billed as "the only fun pub in town", this simple bar attracts an overwhelmingly English crowd. It has pool, Sky TV and, reputedly, the best cocktails in Dalyan. ◈ *Maraş Cad • Map D5*

Left **Grand Bazaar** Right **Netsel Marina**

 Shops

Grand Bazaar, Marmaris
 With a layout reminiscent of an old bazaar, and everything on sale from leather goods to mobile phones and local honey, this is certainly a must for ardent shoppers. ✎ *Kordon Cad • Map P5*

Mısır Çarşisi, Marmaris
A great little shop just outside the bazaar, Mısır Çarşisi stocks a broad range of Turkish natural products. Soap, henna, spices, jams and Turkish delight are among its wares. ✎ *Tepe Mah, 38 Sok • Map P5*

Istanbul Souvenir, Marmaris
Deep within the Grand Bazaar, this small shop is packed with all kinds of souvenirs, from Meerschaum pipes to pretty stained-glass lanterns and Turkish ceramics. ✎ *Tepe Mah 26, Sok 13 • Map P5*

Netsel Marina, Marmaris
Stefanel, Tommy Hilfiger, Fred Perry and Ralph Lauren are among the smart boutiques interspersed with fountains and flowerbeds in this attractive mall within the marina. ✎ *Off Mustafa Münir Elgin Blvd • Map Q5*

Bookstore, Marmaris
Run by a characterful Turkish lady, this tiny bookstore offering a limited range of second-hand English books at reasonable prices is just around the corner from the old mosque. ✎ *Tepe Mah 26, Sok 13 • Map Q4*

Faros Fashion, Marmaris
This well-established leather store in the Grand Bazaar has plenty of "genuine fakes", with frequently updated stock. ✎ *Tepe Mah 57, Sok 22 • Map P5*

Point Centre Mall, Marmaris
This modern, air-conditioned mall close to Long Beach offers all the usual mall experiences – international fast-food outlets, shops and a cinema. ✎ *Kemal Elgin Bulvari, Karacan Plaza 53/101 • Map C4*

Unique Art, Dalyan
Perfect for those in search of unusual jewellery, this small shop is run by the artist who created most of its contents. Many of his pieces are crafted from silver or gold and are Ottoman-influenced. ✎ *Maraş Mah, Maraş Cad 42 • Map D5*

Dalyan Carpets, Dalyan
Part of a cooperative, Dalyan Carpets boasts a stock of more than 5,000 rugs from different parts of Turkey. There's a team of weavers on-site, ready to demonstrate production techniques. ✎ *On the road between Ortaca and Dalyan • Map D5*

Saturday Market, Datça
This is a colourful local market where smallholders from outlying villages fill stalls with their vegetables, almonds, spices, olive oil and herbs, as well as fresh fish and local crafts. ✎ *Datça • Map B5*

Left **Wooden walkway over the water in Saklıkent Gorge** Right **Ölüdeniz beach**

East from Fethiye

Many of ancient Lycia's major settlements, including Xanthos, Patara and Tlos, lay along this section of the coast, which is consequently a treasure-trove of ruins; most famous of all are the spectacular cliff tombs at Kaş and Fethiye. Some sites receive thousands of visitors a year, while others, like Sidyma and Kadyanda, barely register on the tourist radar. The region also boasts some superb beaches – Patara, Kaputaş and Ölüdeniz are among Turkey's best. Anyone interested in getting off the beaten track can follow the Lycian Way, while those in search of a calm base from which to explore the region can try Kaş, Fethiye or Kalkan. For visitors who prefer all-inclusive packages, there are some excellent self-contained resorts scattered along the seaboard.

Lycian tombs cut into the cliffs above Fethiye

Sights

1. Fethiye
2. Kaya Köyü
3. The Lycian Way
4. Ölüdeniz Beach
5. Saklıkent Gorge
6. Xanthos
7. Patara Beach
8. Kalkan
9. Kaş
10. Kekova

Preceding pages **The imposing 2nd-century monumental gateway at Aphrodisias**

Fethiye

1 This attractive town stands on the site of the ancient city of Telmessos, whose natural harbour made it an important Lycian port. The early residents left behind the impressive rock tombs and sarcophagi for which Fethiye is famous today. Until the late 1970s it was a humble fishing town; then the tourists arrived and development began. With plenty of shops and a mellow nightlife scene, it makes a good base from which to explore nearby attractions such as Kaya Köyü and Ölüdeniz beach *(see pp28–9)*.

Kaya Köyü

2 Known as the "Ghost Town", Kaya Köyü is a ruined settlement just outside Fethiye, founded in the 18th century on the site of the ancient city of Karmylassos. It was abandoned by its largely Greek Christian inhabitants in 1923, in the aftermath of the Greco-Turkish War *(see p34)*. The villagers were forcefully moved to Greece, where they were looked upon as Turks and never fully integrated. Today the site is preserved as an open-air museum and attracts large numbers of tourists. Highlights include two Greek Orthodox churches and a 17th-century fountain. ✆ *Map E5*

The "Ghost Town" – Kaya Köyü

The Lycian Way near Çıralı

The Lycian Way

3 Marked in 2000, this 509-km (318-mile) path is Turkey's first long-distance trail. Its official starting point is Ovacık, south of Fethiye, from where it continues across mountains, along deserted beaches and past little-known ruins and isolated villages, eventually culminating near Antalya. Walkers can pick and choose sections of the walk; some are physically challenging or have limited food and water points, so thorough preparation is essential *(see pp20–21)*.

Ölüdeniz Beach

4 One of Turkey's most photographed beaches, this famous stretch of sand attracts many thousands of tourists every year. The sky above is filled with a constant swarm of colourful paragliders, most of whom make tandem-jumps from the summit of nearby Babadağ Mountain for the best views of Ölüdeniz. Though the beach is undoubtedly beautiful, it's worth mentioning the presence of the overdeveloped and rather unattractive resort that has sprung up a short distance away to service the ever-increasing flow of tourists. ✆ *Map E5 • Adm*

The Turkish Santa Claus

The Santa Claus legend is based on St Nicholas – the real-life Bishop of Myra *(see p83)* in the 3rd century AD. He gained his reputation for generosity following a number of good deeds that included giving a bag of gold coins to three sisters after their parents' death, to save them from a life of prostitution. The church of his burial in Demre is a popular pilgrimage site where plastic Santas abound.

Saklıkent Gorge

An enormously popular tourist attraction during the summer months, Saklıkent is Turkey's longest and deepest gorge, measuring 20 km (13 miles) in length and up to 300 m (985 ft) in depth. Entered by a wooden walkway that bears visitors over the torrents exiting the gorge's mouth, a further 4 km (2.5 miles) are walkable through ice-cold water until the smooth limestone walls become too narrow to pass. Water-shoes, which can be rented or bought near the entrance, are essential to avoid slipping on the rocks. There are several opportunities for mud baths along the way. Map E5

Xanthos

In 1988 the Lycian and Roman remains at Xanthos – a settlement dating from the 8th century BC – earned it World Heritage status; but that was too late to save it from English explorer Sir Charles Fellows, who carted off splendid structures such as the Nereid Monument to the British Museum in 1838. Nonetheless, many impressive tombs have survived, along with pillars inscribed with Lycian text and the well-preserved remains of a theatre. Map E6
• Open 9am–7:30pm daily • Adm

Patara Beach

This glorious expanse of sand is not only one of Turkey's best beaches, it's also the site of the city of Patara, which was occupied as early as the Bronze Age and later became a leading Lycian city. Most of the remains lie deep under the sand, but several significant structures have been uncovered. The beach has escaped development due to its vital role as a nesting-ground for endangered loggerhead turtles; it's closed overnight, to allow the turtles to lay their eggs in peace. Map E6 • Open 9am–7pm • Adm

Kalkan

Perched on a steep hillside leading down to a small harbour, this pleasant little fishing town had a largely Greek population until the compulsory population exchange of 1923 *(see p34)*. Today, visitors pass their time at the many stylish bars and restaurants that hug the seafront, or wander the narrow streets lined with the town's characteristic old whitewashed houses, browsing the wares of the many small shops. For the more adventurous, local dive schools organize trips to wrecks and underwater caves in the bay *(see p63)*. Map E6

Kalkan

9 Kaş

Like most of the harbour towns along the coast, Kaş was founded during the Lycian era. Antique tombs mounted on stone pedestals are scattered throughout the town, and majestic rock tombs adorn the cliffs above the bay. Today, Kaş derives most of its income from tourism, and its warren of hilly streets is home to numerous quirky craft shops offering attractive handmade products. There's also a laid-back nightlife scene that revolves around a few characterful bars (see pp30–31).

Boats in the harbour at Kaş

10 Kekova

The sunken ruins off Kekova Island are all that remains of a Lycian settlement razed to the ground by an earthquake during the 2nd century BC. Accessible by boat from the picturesque village of Üçağiz, they consist of ruined foundations, steps cut into the rocks and the wall of a small harbour. It's also possible to visit them by kayak, but swimming and diving is forbidden. The whole area around Üçağiz is littered with sarcophagi and rock tombs belonging to the ancient settlements of Teimiussa and nearby Simena. ◈ Map F6

A Day Out from Fethiye

Morning

For this day trip you'll need your own transport; cars, motorbikes and scooters can be hired for a reasonable price in **Fethiye** (see pp28–9). From the centre, follow signs for Ölüdeniz and continue for 9 km (6 miles) until you reach the bustling inland resort of Hisarönü – there's little to see here, so follow the road as it drops towards **Ölüdeniz** (see p79), 3 km (2 miles) away. Go straight to the beach; there's an entry fee to access the narrow strip of famous sand. Paragliders are a constant presence – tandem flights should be booked a day in advance during high season. Having sampled the turquoise waters, take the road back to Hisarönü and follow signs west to **Kaya Köyü** (see p79), 6 km (4 miles) away. As you enter the village, look out for signs to Kaya Wine House (see p85), where you can treat yourself to a glorious lunch in an atmospheric setting.

Afternoon

Head towards the hillside ruins and enter the site next to the **Levissi Garden** restaurant (see p85). Climb the hill until you reach the High Church, one of the town's two Greek Orthodox churches. Explore the settlement then follow the tiny road as it descends through forests to the secluded **Gemiler Beach**, 3 km (2 miles) away (see p82). Here you can swim, sunbathe or charter a fishing boat to the small island opposite. The tiny seafront restaurant will suffice for dinner before your return to Fethiye.

Left **Kadyanda ruins** Centre **The beach at Gemiler** Right **Ruined fortress and rock tombs at Tlos**

Best of the Rest

1 Kadyanda
Scattered amongst pine trees on a hilltop, the isolated ruins of Kadyanda include a stadium with several rows of seating and a partially excavated 3,500-seat theatre. ✎ Map E5

2 Çalış Beach
Fethiye's main beach lies just north of town. Its 6-km (4-mile) length is lined with umbrellas and backed by hotels, restaurants and bars. ✎ Map E5

3 Gemiler Beach
From this sheltered pebble beach set in a pleasant wooded bay, fishermen shuttle tourists to nearby Gemiler Island. ✎ Map E5

4 Butterfly Valley
The gorgeous beach at the mouth of this isolated valley can only be reached on foot or by boat. Basic camping and catering facilities attract a chilled-out crowd of backpackers. ✎ Map E5

5 Sidyma
The ruins of Sidyma include a necropolis, temple foundations and a tumbledown theatre. The local village mosque is built over the Roman baths. ✎ Map E6

6 Tlos
Tlos is dominated by the hilltop ruins of an Ottoman-era fortress; immediately below are Lycian rock tombs; further down, a Roman stadium and theatre.
✎ Map E5 • Open 9am–7pm daily • Adm

7 Kaputaş Beach
Best viewed from the clifftop road above, this tiny beach is simply stunning. Its golden sands, glistening white pebbles and translucent turquoise waters are picture-postcard material. ✎ Map E6

8 Phellos
This hilltop ruin dating from the 5th century BC is hard to reach and rarely visited, but the glorious views and the large house-tombs near its summit certainly repay the effort. ✎ Map F6

9 St Nicholas Church, Demre (Myra)
Excavated last century, this church is thought to be the burial place of St Nicholas of Myra, progenitor of Santa Claus. In 2007, communion was once again celebrated here, for the first time in centuries. ✎ Map G6 • Open 9am–7pm daily • Adm

10 Elmalı
Set on a high inland plain, Elmalı makes a pleasant day trip to escape the heat of the coast. Highlights are the museum and the rickety Ottoman-era houses of the Old Quarter. ✎ Map G5

Left **Detail of stonework, Myra** Centre **Roman ruins at Patara** Right **Temple remains at Letoon**

Regional Ruins

Patara
Buried under sand for centuries, this great Lycian capital continued to thrive under the Romans. A triumphal arch from AD 100 still stands, along with numerous other structures.
◈ Map E6 • Open 9am–7pm • Adm

Pydnae
Built to guard a Lycian naval base, the substantial remains of this fortress are best reached by boat or on foot. ◈ Map E6

Sura
The jumbled ruins of Sura include a well-preserved Roman mausoleum and a temple of Apollo. In ancient times, its priests divined the future by observing the movements of fish in a sacred pool. ◈ Map F6

Oenoanda
Oenoanda's isolated position has left it virtually untouched by tourists and archaeologists alike, yet these intriguing remains – particularly famous for their lengthy inscriptions of Epicurean philosophy – are well worth a visit. ◈ Map F5

Pinara
Built upon a dramatic rocky crag, the ancient Lycian city of Pinara benefited from superb natural defences. Most intriguing are the small "pigeon-hole" tombs cut into the vertical cliff face, which would only have been accessible by rope ladders. ◈ Map E5

Letoon
A UNESCO World Heritage site, Letoon was primarily a place of worship. The foundations of temples dedicated to the goddess Leto and her children, Apollo and Artemis, are among the most significant remains.
◈ Map E6 • Open 9am–7pm daily • Adm

Af Kule Monastery
Not for vertigo sufferers, this small ruined monastery, clinging dramatically to cliffs high above the sea, comprises several rooms on two levels that can be accessed by rough steps. ◈ Map G6

Myra
Although much of Myra is buried beneath the modern town of Demre, the visible remains, including an ancient Greek theatre and a Lycian necropolis, are striking nonetheless. ◈ Map G6

Dereağzi
Dereağzi's ruined fortress occupies a hilltop overlooking the junction of two rivers. First constructed by the Lycians, it was renovated by the Byzantines, who also built the large church far below. ◈ Map F6

Apollonia
Little is known about this site, which goes by its Greek name as the earlier Lycian name remains unknown. The partially overgrown ruins include a theatre, a reservoir and numerous sarcophagi. ◈ Map F6

Left **Meğri** Right **Paşa Kebap**

🔟 Restaurants in Fethiye

Kale Park
1 Designed to resemble an amphitheatre, Kale Park serves excellent food and has superb views of Fethiye and the bay beyond from its hilltop location. ◈ *Depboy Mevkii, Kaya Yolu • Map E5 • (0252) 612 91 19 • €€*

Arena Terrace
2 The perfect spot for a quiet dinner, this smart restaurant with good food and a lengthy wine list occupies a first-floor terrace beside the amphitheatre. ◈ *Karagozler 1, Paspatur Giriş • Map E5 • (0252) 612 00 54 • Open year-round • €€€*

Mod Yacht Lounge
3 This place is popular with yachters for the wide choice of breakfasts, some lovely Turkish and international dishes, and regular barbecue nights in the secluded garden. ◈ *Fethiye Marina • Map E5 • (0252) 614 39 70 • €€€€*

Hilmi
4 One of the many restaurants forming a circle around the lively fish market, Hilmi stands out with its crisp white tablecloths. Pick your fish and send it straight to the chef. ◈ *Hal ve Pazar Yeri 53 • Map E5 • (0252) 612 62 42 • €€€€*

Megri
5 A popular eatery within the bazaar, Meğri's menu includes Turkish salads, grilled meat and *kebaps*, as well as steak, pizza and pasta. ◈ *Çarsi Cad 26 • Map E5 • (0252) 614 40 40 • €€*

Nefis Pide
6 A generous choice of *pide* (a Turkish version of pizza made with flat bread) and good kebabs make this a great venue for a cheap lunch. ◈ *Eski Cami Sok 9 • Map E5 • (0252) 614 55 04 • Open year-round • €*

Şamdan
7 Hidden away down a side street and mostly frequented by locals, Şamdan is a good place to sample meze *(see p53)*. ◈ *Tütün Sok 9 • Map E5 • (0252) 614 28 68 • Open year-round • €€*

Çitir
8 This well-established fish-market restaurant will prepare your chosen fish whichever way you prefer; or select from the international menu, with such favourites as pepper steak and beef curry. ◈ *Hal ve Pazar Yeri 38 • Map E5 • (0252) 614 64 94 • €€*

The Duck Pond
9 Squeezed between a rough brick wall and the bazaar's duck-filled pond, this atmospheric outdoor restaurant whose walls are decorated with colourful local artwork specializes in casseroles and stir-fries. ◈ *Çarsi Cad 24 • Map E5 • (0252) 614 74 29 • €€*

Paşa Kebap
10 This simple restaurant serves superb *kebaps* and salads and has earned itself a reputation for friendly service, cleanliness and great value. ◈ *Çarsi Cad 42 • Map E5 • (0252) 614 98 07 • Open year-round • €€*

Restaurants are open between early April and late October unless otherwise stated.

Price Categories

For a three-course meal for one with half a bottle of wine (or equivalent meal), taxes and extra charges.

€ under €15
€€ €15–€25
€€€ €25–€30
€€€€ €30–€35
€€€€€ over €35

Levissi Garden, Kaya Köyü

🔟 Restaurants Beyond Fethiye

1 Kaya Wine House, Kaya Köyü

Hidden away down a tiny rural lane, this hugely atmospheric family-run restaurant serves wonderful home-cooked food and exquisite local wines. ⊗ *Gökçeburun Mah 70 • Map E5 • (0252) 618 04 54 • €€€*

2 Levissi Garden, Kaya Köyü

Diners can choose between Turkish and international dishes at this large, centrally located Ottoman-style restaurant with a vast wine cellar. ⊗ *Beside entrance to ruined town • Map E5 • (0252) 618 01 08 • €€€€*

3 Çin Bal, Kaya Köyü

At Çin Bal, diners select their raw meat from a refrigerated display, then cook it themselves on a portable barbecue. ⊗ *Off Hisarönü Cad • Map E5 • (0252) 618 00 66 • €€*

4 Coast@Gironda, Kalkan

High-class fusion cuisine is on offer at this sophisticated restaurant, with plush seating in a secluded garden or on a terrace with sweeping sea views. ⊗ *Hasan Altan Cad • Map E6 • (0242) 844 12 98 • €€€€€€*

5 Belgin's Kitchen, Kalkan

Perfect for an authentic Turkish dining experience. Diners sit cross-legged on cushions at low tables in a converted barn. *Manti* (Turkish ravioli) is among the typical dishes. ⊗ *Yaliboyu 1 • Map E6 • (0242) 844 36 14 • €€€*

6 Aubergine, Kalkan

This well-established seafront restaurant and cocktail bar offers a good selection of the owner's favourite aubergine-based dishes. ⊗ *Kalkan Marina • Map E6 • (0242) 844 33 32 • €€€€*

7 Chez Evy, Kaş

Renowned for its superb French cuisine, Chez Evy's menu features wild boar, steak and succulent lamb, along with delicious desserts. ⊗ *Terzi Sok 4 • Map F6 • (0242) 836 12 53 • Open year-round • €€€€€*

8 Mercan, Kaş

Mercan is certainly the place for fresh, high-quality fish, and the spectacle of its chefs vigorously gutting and slicing the day's catch attracts both diners and onlookers. ⊗ *Balıkçı Barinaği, Kaş Marina • Map F6 • (0242) 836 12 09 • €€€€*

9 Buzz Beach Bar, Ölüdeniz

One of many restaurants along the bustling beachfront, Buzz serves old favourites like fish and chips and spaghetti bolognaise. Diners can chill out on the shaded terrace. ⊗ *Ölüdeniz Beach • Map E5 • (0252) 617 05 26 • €€*

10 Kanyon, Saklıkent

If you can brave the rickety bridge, dining at tables perched just above the rushing Saklıkent river is the perfect way to cool off after a long walk in the gorge. ⊗ *Next to the mouth of Saklıkent Gorge • Map E5 • (0252) 659 00 89 • €€*

Left **Theatre at Termessos** Right **Finike Marina**

South from Antalya

In complete contrast to the westward route, the road south of Antalya winds through a pristine landscape of verdant mountains, with glimpses of the sea and unspoiled beaches far below. Much of the region has benefited from being part of the Beydağları National Park, and many of its beaches have been saved by their status as nesting-grounds for endangered loggerhead turtles. Kemer, the only resort of significant size on this stretch of the coast, is attractive and thoughtfully planned, while Çıralı offers independent visitors rural calm and tranquillity beside one of the coast's loveliest beaches. This is also a great region for hiking – the Lycian Way follows a route that encompasses both mountains and beaches. Anyone preferring the easy option can take the cable car to the top of Mount Olympos.

Yacht harbour at Antalya

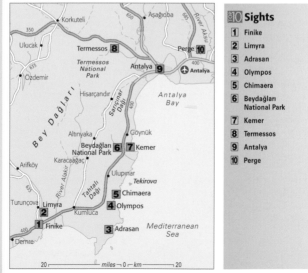

Sights

1. Finike
2. Limyra
3. Adrasan
4. Olympos
5. Chimaera
6. Beydağları National Park
7. Kemer
8. Termessos
9. Antalya
10. Perge

Finike

Originally named Phoenicus, after its Phoenician founders, Finike started life in the 5th century BC. For centuries it was an important Lycian trading port. Nowadays it's a bustling little town with neat parks, a couple of pebble beaches and a well-established marina. The town derives much of its income from the production of oranges, so although it attracts a steady flow of Turkish and foreign visitors, it isn't solely dependent on their custom, and there has been less development here than at some other coastal towns.  Map G6

Beach at Adrasan

Limyra

Chosen as the capital of Lycia in the 4th century BC, Limyra remained a powerful city until its demise around the 9th century AD. Its five necropolises, featuring hundreds of graves both freestanding and cut into the rock face, underline its status, as do the many fine buildings erected by its wealthy citizens. The remains of a Bishop's church and palace prove its continuing influence into the Christian era. A short walk east of Limyra is the late-Roman Limyra Bridge – one of the oldest segmented-arch bridges in the world. Map G6

Ruins of Limyra

Adrasan

Lying in an idyllic sheltered bay with a marvellous sandy beach, this tiny resort's proximity to the Beydağları National Park has ensured that development has remained minimal. The few large hotels are far outnumbered by small pensions and laid-back beachfront cafés and restaurants. Visitors who tire of swimming and sunbathing can try their hand at waterskiing, parasailing or banana-boating; the bay also has some good diving spots (see p63). Map H6

Olympos

A short hike up the coast from Adrasan, the overgrown ruins of Olympos are an intriguing sight, occupying a picturesque location at the mouth of a small river whose waters flow into the crystal-clear Mediterranean beyond. In ancient Greek and Roman times, boats docked at the quay on the river's south bank, and traces of this dock can clearly be seen today. Equally famous are the treehouse complexes that have sprung up along the valley, attracting a steady flow of hedonistic backpackers to the area. Map H6

Overgrown ruins of Olympos

Beydağlari National Park

Hikers can explore the region by
following the Çıralı section of the
well-marked Lycian Way trail (see
pp20–21). ◈ Map H5

Chimaera
Taking their name from the
Chimaera, a fire-breathing monster
of Greek mythology, the flames
that flicker enchantingly from the
rock face in the hills above Çıralı
are caused by a natural
phenomenon that has
yet to be explained
fully. Best visited after
dark, excursions are
organized from both
Çıralı and Olympos.
The flames are reached
by a stony footpath
from the car park –
stout shoes and a
torch are recommen-
ded. ◈ Map H6 • Adm

Chimaera

Beydağları National Park
A broad swathe of land
south of Antalya, Beydağları
National Park encompasses both
the Tahtalı and Sarıçınar Dağı
mountain ranges, along with many
coastal areas. It is home to bears,
wolves, jackals, wild boars and
more than a thousand species of
plant, as well as the endangered
green and loggerhead turtles that
nest at Çıralı beach. Highlights of
the park include Göynük Canyon
(see p36), Olympos and Chimaera.

Kemer
Surrounded by high, forested
mountains, Kemer is a refresh-
ingly well-planned resort with
low buildings, wide streets, pretty
fountains and an abundance of
greenery. The big resort hotels
are kept at bay on
the periphery of town,
while the centre is
taken up with small
shops and restaurants.
Hugely popular with
Russian package tour-
ists, the resort has a
reputation for a frenetic
nightlife that focuses
on two neighbouring
clubs on the outskirts. The large
and well-equipped marina is a
popular stop-off for yachts and
boat tours. ◈ Map H5

Termessos
It's easy to understand why
Alexander the Great decided
against launching an attack on
this seemingly impenetrable city,
set high on a wooded plateau
and defended by a complex
arrangement of fortified walls.
Termessos flourished during the
Roman era, when it minted its
own coins and erected numerous

impressive buildings. Significant remains are easily seen, but much of the site is being lost to dense undergrowth *(see pp12–13).*

Antalya

Dating back to the 2nd century BC, Antalya has thrived under a succession of dynasties, each of which has left its mark – most notably on the Old Town, Kaleiçi (literally, "the inner castle"). The undisputed capital of Turkey's Mediterranean coast, this ever-expanding city processes millions of tourists annually through its airport. Most head for resorts to the east and south, but many stay to experience the calm of the seaside parks, the charm of shopping in Kaleiçi or the fascination of the remains on display at one of the country's best museums *(see pp8–11).*

Perge

Like most of the ancient Anatolian cities, Perge reached the height of its fame and prosperity under Roman rule during the first three centuries AD. Today, its most impressive remains are a remarkably intact colonnaded street that was once lined with shops, and the ruins of a pair of grand towers that flanked the city gate. Many of the intricately carved sarcophagi discovered at Perge are now on display at Antalya's archaeological museum. ⊗ *Map J4 • Open 8:30am–6pm daily • Adm*

Colonnaded street in the agora, Perge

Exploring Antalya's Old Town

Morning

🕒 Start outside the Old Town (Kaleiçi) at **Hadrian's Gate**. *(see p9).* Pass through the gate and turn right onto Imaret Sokak. Follow the street until it brings you to a junction with the **Tekeli Mehmet Paşa Mosque** *(see p9)* on the left and the **Clock Tower** *(see p8)* on the right. You can either visit **Yivli Minaret** *(see p8),* visible above the buildings opposite, or turn left onto Uzun Çarşı Sokak, one of the main shopping streets, which draws you into the depths of the Old Town. Turn into Balıkpazarı Sokak, the fourth street on the left after the mosque, and follow it to the end, where a right turn takes you down a long street past an over-grown Ottoman mansion to the harbour; here, the **Mermerli Restaurant** *(see p92)* makes a great lunch-stop, with lovely sea views.

Afternoon

From the Mermerli, you can either climb down the steps to explore the harbour, or follow the road back up the hill. If you opt for the latter, take the first right and keep turning right along the winding streets until you reach Hıdırlık Sokak, from where you can follow signs to the ancient **Hıdırlık Tower** *(see p9).* Then, either wander into the delightful **Karaalioğlu Park** *(see p9),* or follow Hesapçi Sokak to see the intriguing **Korkut Minaret** *(see p9).* Continuing along the narrow street will bring you back to Hadrian's Gate, from where it's just a short stroll to the left along Atatürk Caddesi to a covered area of kebab restaurants for a well-deserved meal.

Left **Cable car to Mount Olympos** Right **Olympia Tree Houses, Çıralı**

TOP10 Best of the Rest

1 Arykanda
Set on rocky cliffs high in the Bey Mountains, Arykanda's most impressive remains are a small theatre and temples dedicated to the god Helios and the Roman Emperor Trajan. ✆ *Map G5 • (0242) 238 56 88 • Open 9am–7pm daily • Adm*

2 Gelidonya Lighthouse
An easy two-and-a-half hour trek from the village of Karaöz, this working lighthouse occupies a splendidly isolated spot on Cape Gelidonya, a stop along the Lycian Way *(see pp20–21)* and a great place for a picnic. ✆ *Map H6*

3 Olympos Teleferik
Large cable-car cabins whisk passengers up to the summit of Mount Olympos for glorious views from its observation platforms. ✆ *Map H6 • (0242) 242 22 52 • Open 9am–7pm daily • Adm • Café • www. olymposteleferik.com*

4 Ulupınar
Nestled in a rocky valley near Ulupınar village are a dozen or so fish restaurants with tables poised precariously over the Ulupınar River. ✆ *Map H5*

5 Çıralı
This wonderfully sleepy cluster of over 50 small palm-shaded pensions, tree houses, restaurants and camp-sites is just a stone's throw from a superb beach. ✆ *Map H6*

6 Phaselis
One of the coast's most beautifully situated ruins, Phaselis was founded in 690 BC and developed into a prosperous trading port. ✆ *Map H5 • (0242) 238 56 88 • Open 8:30am–6pm daily • Adm • Café*

7 Three Islands, Tekirova
Just off the coast from the resort of Tekirova are several islands with fantastic diving opportunities that include two underwater caves, nine reefs and a deep canyon. ✆ *Map H6*

8 Karain Cave, Yağca Köyü
Located high on a hillside overlooking a broad plain, this cave, with its dramatic sculpted interior, is thought to have been continuously inhabited from the Paleolithic Era to Byzantine times. ✆ *Map H4 • (0242) 238 56 88 • Open 9am–7pm daily • Adm*

9 Konyaaltı Beach, Antalya
Antalya's enormously popular beach has earned a Blue Flag Award for beach- and water-quality, and stretches for an umbrella-infested 7 km (4 miles) southwest of the city *(see pp8–9)*.

10 Kursunlu Falls
A short trip from Antalya, the Kursunlu Falls are set amidst lush vegetation. Visitors can picnic right beside them. ✆ *Map J4*

Some finds from Karain Cave are on display in its small museum; more can be seen at Antalya Archaeological Museum (see pp10–11).

Left **Club Ally, Antalya** Right **Club Arma, Antalya**

🔟 Nightlife

1 Club Ally, Antalya
Ally occupies a superb spot within the walls of the old town. A thumping sound system, state-of-the-art lighting, dancing girls and prohibitively expensive drinks make this the place to be seen in Antalya. ⬎ *Selçuk Mah, Sur Sok no. 4/8, Kaleiçi • Map N2 • Adm*

2 Club Arma, Antalya
This exclusive club and restaurant set on a rocky promontory beside the old harbour pumps out the latest pop tunes accompanied by choking clouds of dry ice and scantily-clad dancers. ⬎ *Kaleiçi Yat Limanı, İskele Cad 75 • Map N2*

3 Club Aura, Kemer
An open-air club on the beachfront, Club Aura competes with its neighbour, Inferno, to bring in the hottest international DJs, often from Russia, to please the overwhelmingly Russian crowd. ⬎ *Deniz Cad 3 • Map H5*

4 Club Inferno, Kemer
Inferno plays hi-energy pop and techno tunes to crowds of eager Russian tourists. There are foam parties several nights a week. ⬎ *Deniz Cad 1 • Map H5*

5 King Bar, Antalya
The city's quirkiest rock bar has wooden beer barrels for tables and the front end of a car over the bar, among other odd details. Expect a warm welcome from the friendly staff. ⬎ *Kaleiçi Marina 11 • Map N2*

6 Jolly Joker Pub, Antalya
Not to be confused with the Jolly Joker restaurant across the road, this capacious rock bar above Starbucks gets very lively, with local rock bands playing most nights. ⬎ *İsmet Gökşen Cad, Lider Plaza 10/13 • Map H5*

7 Çiçek Pasaji, Antalya
Tucked away behind old stone walls, Çiçek Pasaji is a great place to catch traditional Turkish music played live. ⬎ *Uzun Carsi Sok 24–26, Kaleiçi • Map P1*

8 Bambus Beach Club, Antalya
By day, this seafront spot operates as a restaurant and beach club; by night, it becomes an exclusive club with a dance floor right by the sea. ⬎ *Yeşilbahçe Mah Eski Lara Yolu No1 • Map H5*

9 Kadir's Treehouse Club, Olympos
Part of the legendary Treehouse complex, this partially covered club features an earthen floor with a blazing bonfire at its centre. Local DJs keep neighbouring tree-house dwellers awake with old favourites that reverberate throughout the valley. ⬎ *Map H6*

10 Retro Club, Antalya
This funky bar-cum-club with mismatched furniture, rickety bookcases and furry wallpaper has live rock music most nights. The clientèle is eclectic. ⬎ *Uzun Çarşi Sok 14, Kaleiçi • Map P2*

Left **Castle Restaurant** Centre **Marina Residence** Right **Hasanağa**

TOP 10 Restaurants in Antalya

1 Divan Antalya Teras Restaurant

One of several restaurants in the Divan Antalya Hotel, the Teras offers unrivalled sea views and an exquisite choice of Turkish and Mediterranean cuisine.
Ⓢ *Divan Antalya Hotel, Fevzi Çakmak Cad 30 • Map H5 • (0242) 248 68 00 • Open year-round • €€€€€*

2 Marina Residence

Located in an elegantly restored 19th-century mansion, the plush Residence serves a select choice of Turkish and international dishes. Ⓢ *Mermerli Sok 15, Kaleiçi • Map N3 • (0242) 247 54 90 • Open year-round • €€€€*

3 Tuti

Expect artfully presented and innovative dishes from the award-winning team of chefs at the Marmara Hotel. Ⓢ *Marmara Hotel, Sirinyali Mah, Lara • Map H5 • (0242) 249 36 00 • €€€€€*

4 Villa Perla

This delightful restaurant serves traditional Turkish cuisine in the tree-shaded grounds of a restored Ottoman mansion. Ⓢ *Villa Perla Hotel, Hesapçi Sok 26, Kaleiçi • Map P1 • (0242) 248 97 93 • €€€€*

5 Antalya Balik Evi

This hugely popular fish restaurant has a predictably broad range of fresh seafood, a pleasant garden and excellent service. Ⓢ *Eski Lara Yolu • Map H5 • (0242) 323 18 23 • €€€€€*

6 Secret Garden (Gizli Bahçe)

Tucked away behind the walls of the Old Town, Secret Garden has panoramic views and a lovely selection of favourite local dishes.
Ⓢ *Selçuk Mah, Dizdar Hasan Bey Sok 1 • Map N2 • (0242) 244 80 10 • €€€€*

7 Hasanağa

Set in a large, vine-shaded courtyard surrounded by old stone walls, the atmospheric Hasanağa offers plenty of fish options as well as traditional Turkish cuisine. Ⓢ *Tuzcular Mah, Mescit Sok 15 • Map P2 • (0242) 242 81 05 • €€*

8 Akdeniz Çiçek Pasaji

Occupying a snug spot beneath the Old Town walls, this restaurant serves well-prepared Turkish dishes at reasonable prices. Ⓢ *Uzun Carsi Sok 24–6, Kaleiçi • Map P1 • (0242) 243 43 03 • €*

9 Castle Restaurant

This simple restaurant with a good range of Turkish dishes has sweeping sea views from high on the clifftop by Hırdırlık Tower *(see p9)*. Ⓢ *Hıdırlık Sok 48/1, Kaleiçi • Map N3 • (0242) 242 31 88 • €€*

10 Mermerli Restaurant

Perched atop the cliffs of the Old Harbour, Mermerli's terrace is a great place to enjoy grilled meats and freshly caught fish. There's also exclusive access to a private beach below.
Ⓢ *Selçuk Mah, Mermerli Banyo Sok 25, Kaleiçi • Map N2 • (0242) 316 53 07 • €€*

Restaurants are open between early April and late October unless otherwise stated.

Price Categories

For a three-course meal for one with half a bottle of wine (or equivalent meal), taxes and extra charges.	
€	under €15
€€	€15–€25
€€€	€25–€30
€€€€	€30–€35
€€€€€	over €35

Şelale Restaurant, Ulupınar

🔟 Restaurants Beyond Antalya

1 Şelale Restaurant, Ulupınar

At one of Ulupınar's most remarkable fish restaurants, numerous low dining platforms straddle the river as it cascades noisily over mossy boulders. ⊗ *Map H5 • (0242) 825 00 25 • €€*

2 Karakuş Restaurant, Çıralı

Of the many restaurants lining the glorious beachfront at Çıralı, Karakuş is perhaps the smartest. Freshly caught fish are on display. ⊗ *Çıralı beachfront • Map H6 • (0242) 825 72 75 • €€*

3 Botanik Restaurant, Ulupınar

Botanik offers superb baked trout from its own trout farm as well as a broad range of Turkish dishes. Guests can fish for their trout. ⊗ *Map H5 • (0242) 825 00 13 • €€€*

4 Monte Kemer Restaurant, Kemer

This clean, family-run restaurant offers sushi and international dishes as well as Turkish cuisine and a good selection of Anatolian wines. ⊗ *Atatürk Cad 41/B • Map H5 • (0242) 814 29 97 • €€€*

5 Chill House Lounge, Adrasan

As laid-back as the name would suggest, Chill House has soft cushions, drapes and mellow vibes aplenty – complemented by Turkish food, pizza, pasta and steak. ⊗ *Deniz Yolu • Map H6 • (0532) 775 26 18 (mobile) • €€*

6 Petek Restaurant, Finike

This well-established restaurant overlooking the marina has long been a favourite of visiting yachters and locals alike. Fresh fish and generous portions are the order of the day. ⊗ *Liman Girisi • Map G6 • (0242) 855 50 29 • €€*

7 Navigator Restaurant, Kemer

Occupying a broad, shaded terrace facing the harbour, Navigator has a decent range of fresh fish options as well as a selection of international dishes. ⊗ *Kemer Marina • Map H5 • (0242) 814 14 90 • €€€€*

8 Mr Frog Pub, Kemer

Popular with Russian tourists, this relaxed place features Mexican, Chinese, Italian and Turkish dishes, among others. Karaoke most nights. ⊗ *Deniz Cad 42 • Map H5 • (0242) 814 36 42 • €€€€*

9 Orange Home, Çıralı

Huge wooden umbrellas shade tables in the sand right by the sea at Çıralı beach. The restaurant specializes in fresh fish, Turkish cuisine and various kinds of casserole. ⊗ *Beachfront • Map H6 • (0242) 825 72 93 • €€*

10 Ceneviz, Adrasan

The menu at this pleasant family-run restaurant features such international favourites as "egg 'n' chips", along with Turkish specialities including Hot Adana Kebab. ⊗ *Beachfront • Map H6 • (0242) 883 10 30 • €€*

Left **Street scene, Side** Right **Gloria golf course, Belek**

West from Alanya

*O*nce the haven of slave traders and pirates who built heavily defended
settlements, this stretch of coastline is now the preserve of developers
who seem intent on constructing their own modern-day wall of monolithic
hotels, apartment blocks and shops to serve the ever-increasing flow of
Russian, German and Scandinavian sun-worshippers. Despite this rampant
development, the sea still sparkles and the beaches remain stunning; the
ruins at Side, Alanya and Aspendos are as striking as ever; and there are
enchanting caves, canyons and waterfalls waiting
to be explored. For those craving excitement, an
enormous range of activities is on offer – from
scuba diving and parasailing to jeep safaris.

Sights

1 Köprülü Canyon National Park
2 Rafting
3 Aspendos
4 Belek
5 Side
6 Manavgat Falls
7 Seleukia
8 Damlataş Cave
9 Alanya
10 Dim Cave

Cleopatra beach, Alanya

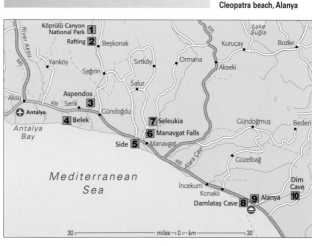

Preceding pages **The Aegean Sea washing round the tip of
Ölüdeniz beach into the blue lagoon beyond**

1 Köprülü Canyon National Park

Overshadowed by the Dedegöl Mountains to the east and the Kuyucak range to the west, this 146-sq-km (56-sq-mile) park is popular with both hikers and rafters. It is densely forested with Mediterranean cypress and home to numerous animal species including deer, wild boars, wolves, bears, foxes, eagles and hawks. The canyon itself is a fissure in the park's limestone floor that runs for 14 km (9 miles) to the sea. It's up to 100 m (328 ft) wide and 400 m (1,312 ft) deep in places, and is traversed by two intact Roman bridges. ✆Map J4

2 Rafting

Anyone interested in experiencing the thrill of white-water rafting in a beautiful setting should head straight for Köprülü Canyon or book a tour with one of the many agencies operating out of Alanya, Side and Manavgat. Rafters get kitted out

Theatre at Aspendos

with wetsuits and helmets before being carried away by the Köprü River as it rushes down from the Taurus Mountains through narrow gorges and past sheer cliff faces. Suitable for beginners, the rapids are rated as Class I and Class II. ✆ Map J4
• Open May–Oct • www.raftingantalya.com

3 Aspendos

Aspendos is thought to have been founded some time in the 8th century BC. It was one of the first ancient cities in the region to begin minting its own coins, but it wasn't until the 2nd century AD that its magnificent theatre was built. By far the best-preserved theatre in Turkey, it has 41 rows of seats with a total capacity of around 8,000 spectators, who would have purchased clay tickets printed with seat numbers for each event. Today the theatre is regularly used to host performances. ✆Map J4
• 8:30am–6pm • Adm

4 Belek

This purpose-built 5-star golf resort was established in the mid-1980s. It now has 14 international-standard golf courses beautifully landscaped and set amidst mature pine forests. Access to the courses is normally through a package deal with associated hotels, but players can also use them on a daily basis. The most challenging are the 27-hole Faldo course, the Montgomerie and the PGA Sultan, while the Pasha and Gloria courses are more suitable for average golfers. ✆Map J5
• (0242) 312 04 44 • www.golfturkey.com

Rafting at Köprülü Canyon

The theatre at Aspendos is thought to have been built around AD 155 by the Greek architect Zenon.

5 Side

The intriguing ruins of Side (pronounced *see-deh*) sprawl over a flat peninsula that was once heavily defended by towers, ramparts and thick stone walls. Probably founded around the 7th century BC, the town briefly prospered as a slave-trading centre before the Roman period, when a huge theatre, temples and fine houses were built. As the Empire weakened, Side fell on hard times. Today, the tip of the peninsula is taken up with a pleasant pedestrianized quarter of shops, guest houses and restaurants *(see pp22–3)*.

6 Manavgat Falls

Hundreds of boats line the riverside at Manavgat, ready to take tourists on the 3-km (2-mile) trip up the broad Manavgat River to the falls (which are famous enough to have featured on a Turkish banknote in the 1970s). Though only 5 m (16 ft) high, they are wide, and the sheer volume of water gushing over the edge is impressive; a restaurant perched on the river bank offers diners a great view. Ⓢ Map K5 • Adm

Ruins at Seleukia

Manavgat Falls

Pirates of Alanya

Following the defeat by Roman forces of the ambitious Seleucid ruler Antiochus III (241–187 BC) in 191 BC, a brief political vacuum in Alanya was rapidly filled by pirates. They built heavily defended bases and terrorized the Mediterranean for centuries. When their activities began to hinder trade with Rome, a succession of battles culminated in their defeat in 70 BC at the hands of the legendary Roman general, Pompeius Magnus (106–48 BC).

7 Seleukia

Half hidden by pine forests, the ruins of ancient Seleukia are, in part, surprisingly well-preserved. One wall of the town's large two-storey bathhouse is relatively intact, and many of the columns that once formed a colonnaded street are still standing today. A bronze statue of Apollo and a pair of mosaics – one depicting Orpheus charming the wild beasts and the other showing famous thinkers of antiquity – were discovered in Seleukia's *agora* (marketplace); they are now on permanent display at Antalya Archaeological Museum *(see pp10–11)*. Ⓢ Map K5

8 Damlataş Cave

Smaller than Dim Cave *(see opposite)*, but more easily accessible, Damlataş Cave lies on the western side of Alanya's rocky outcrop, and can be entered from Cleopatra Beach. Discovered in 1948 during building work on the harbour,

a passage leads visitors 50 m (164 ft) into the rock, where they enter caverns populated by the 15,000-year-old stalactites and stalagmites from which the cave got its name; Damlataş means "dripping stone" in Turkish. The dank atmosphere of the cave – which combines high levels of humidity and carbon dioxide – is said to be beneficial for asthma sufferers. ◎ Map L5
• Open 9am–6pm daily • Adm

9 Alanya

This thriving resort has been relentlessly developed, but it still retains some historic charm thanks to the old castle walls, whose remains snake over the rocky promontory beside which the modern city is set. The Scandinavian, German and Russian tourists who pour in every season in their thousands are generally more interested in Alanya's other assets: a pair of superb beaches, more than 250 sunny days a year, inexhaustible shopping opportunities and some of the best nightlife on the south coast (see pp24–5).

10 Dim Cave

The result of millions of years of water erosion from rain and melting snow, this spectacular cave is located high in the mountains above the Dimçay River. Visitors enter the gloomy interior, which remains at a constant 18–19° C (64–66° F), and follow a 350-m (1,148-ft) walkway that passes through a series of limestone caverns. Here there are huge stalactites and stalagmites, columns, travertine pools and a 17-m- (56-ft-) deep lake. The viewing platform by the entrance offers sweeping vistas of the surrounding mountains. ◎ Map L5 • Open 9am–6pm • Adm

Alanya in a Day

Morning

Start with a visit to Alanya's excellent **museum** (see pp24, 25), to get a picture of the town's colourful history. After that, cross to the **Tourist Information Centre** (see p24) on the corner of Damlataş Caddesi, from where a half-hourly bus whisks visitors up to the **castle** (kale) (see p24) at the top of Alanya's great rocky outcrop. Any of the simple cafés scattered around the entrance will be perfect for a refreshment break. Explore the castle ruins and enjoy breathtaking panoramic views from the ramparts. Walk back down the road and follow the signs off to the left to the **Suleymaniye Mosque** (see p24), from where you can explore the narrow streets of the Old Town. Return to the main road and stop for lunch on the right-hand side at the **Kale Panorama** restaurant (see p102), with unrivalled views of the harbour and eastern Alanya.

Afternoon

The castle road brings you to the harbour, where a visit to the intriguing **Red Tower** (see p24) is a must. Nearby, you can board a small fishing boat for a one-hour trip that takes in **Tersane** (see p25), the old shipyard where Selçuk warships were built; **Pirate's Cave** (see p100); and Phosphorus Cave, where a mysterious light shimmers from under the water. Back on dry land, wander north along the harbour to the covered bazaar for some shopping, before dinner at the popular **Queen's Garden** restaurant (see p102). If you still have the energy, party the night away at any of the nearby clubs.

Left **Manavgat Falls** Right **The beach at İncekum**

TOP 10 Best of the Rest

1 Sillyon
Less well preserved than nearby Perge, hilltop Sillyon is an appealing ruin nonetheless. It was one of the few towns in the region that managed to repel an attack from Alexander the Great in the 4th century BC. ⬥ Map J4

2 Birdwatching, Belek
The Belek region is not only a paradise for golfers, but a Mecca for birdwatchers too – over 100 of Turkey's 450 bird species can be spotted in the area. ⬥ Map J5

3 Selge
Situated high in the hills and some distance inland, Selge prospered during the Roman era as an independent town that traded in olive oil and minted its own coins. ⬥ Map J4

4 Manavgat
The main attractions of this bustling inland town are its broad river (overlooked by pleasant restaurants) and the famous waterfall a short distance upstream (see p98). ⬥ Map K5

5 Alarahan
Alaeddin Keykubad was the sultan responsible for the artistic and architectural regeneration of Alanya in the 13th century. His caravanserai at Alarahan was built to serve as an inn for traders travelling between Konya and Alanya. The building has since been restored, and now houses several souvenir shops. ⬥ Map K5

6 İncekum
This family-friendly resort occupies a lovely sandy bay with shallow sea that's perfect for young children. ⬥ Map K5

7 Sorgun Beach
Enduringly popular, this broad expanse of clean golden sand has escaped the ravages of overdevelopment. ⬥ Map L5

8 Hamaxia
This hillside settlement provided timber for the Roman ship-building industry. Remains include a well, a fountain and a necropolis. ⬥ Map L5

9 Colybrassus
Little is known about these scattered ruins beyond their Roman origins. Among the most distinctive remains are a temple and the city wall. ⬥ Map L5

10 Pirate's Cave Boat Trip, Alanya
One of several of Alanya's caves, Pirate's Cave can only be entered in one of the small fishing boats that run tours from the harbour.
⬥ Alanya • Map L5 • 9am–6pm • Adm

Left **Havana Club, Alanya** Right **James Dean Bar, Alanya**

Nightlife

1 Robin Hood Bar, Alanya
One of the focal points of Alanya's frenetic nightlife, Robin Hood offers four floors of rock, retro, pop and dance music, along with foam parties and a roof terrace overlooking the harbour. ◊ *Iskele Cad • Map L5*

2 Havana Club, Alanya
Located on Cleopatra beach some distance from the centre of Alanya, Havana serves up noisy dance tunes and great cocktails to an ecstatic crowd until 3am, seven days a week. ◊ *Hükümet Cad 13 • Map L6*

3 Auditorium Club, Alanya
When most of Alanya's clubs shut down at 3am, Auditorium, the town's largest, sends out a free double-decker bus to pull in punters for another three hours of sweaty partying. ◊ *Dimçayi Quarter • Map L5*

4 James Dean Bar, Alanya
This stylish nightclub squeezed between Robin Hood and Bistrot Bellman has two floors and a large open terrace with male podium dancers. ◊ *Iskele Cad • Map L5*

5 Bistro Bellman, Alanya
A grandly styled open-air club fronted with Roman arches and columns, Bistro Bellman operates as a restaurant by day before its transformation into one of Alanya's nightlife hot spots. ◊ *Iskele Cad • Map L5*

6 Apollo Club, Side
Bizarrely located within the ruins surrounding the temple of Apollo in Side *(see pp22–3)*, this latter-day Apollo plays a mix of rock and pop tunes to a merry crowd of modern worshippers. ◊ *Ceylan Cad • Map K5*

7 Lighthouse Club, Side
Occupying a prime spot jutting out into Side harbour, the smartly furnished Lighthouse opens every evening for Italian food, followed by a club night of the latest pop and dance tunes. ◊ *Liman Cad • Map K5*

8 The Doors Rock Bar, Alanya
This cramped first-floor bar plays loud rock music to euphoric crowds of blond Scandinavians. It's sweaty, claustrophobic and great fun. ◊ *Iskele Cad • Map L5*

9 Kiss Café Bar, Manavgat
Kiss is a pleasant spot to wind down after a hard day's sightseeing. On offer are comfy seating, great views and a reasonable range of cocktails and snacks. ◊ *Barbaros Cad 64 • Map K5*

10 Cumbus Café Bar, Manavgat
Favoured by local youngsters, this funky modern establishment is squeezed in amongst the cafés and shops on Manavgat's suspension bridge. It stays open until late and has occasional live music. ◊ *Asma Köprü Ustü • Map K5*

Left **Ottoman House** Centre **Janus Bar** Right **Redtower Brewery**

🔟 Restaurants in Alanya

1 Ottoman House
Sample traditional Turkish cuisine in this excellent restaurant set in a beautifully restored mansion with lush gardens. ◈ *Damlataş Cad 31 • Map L5 • (0242) 511 14 21 • €€€€*

2 Kale Panorama
Overlooking the harbour from a superb vantage point halfway up the rocky outcrop *(see p24)*, Kale Panorama occupies a series of shaded terraces. The menu is international. ◈ *Castle Cad 15 • Map L5 • (0242) 512 62 82 • €€€*

3 Green Beach Restaurant
This delightful restaurant with palm-shaded seating right beside the beach offers a wide choice of dishes and wines. Service is polite and efficient. ◈ *Güzelyari Cad 33 • Map L5 • (0242) 512 54 89 • €€€€€*

4 Janus Bar
Set on the harbour front with a broad, shaded terrace, Janus serves a good range of fresh fish and international dishes by day. At night, it morphs into a hedonistic party spot. ◈ *Iskele Cad 30 • Map L5 • (0242) 513 26 94 • €€€*

5 Queen's Garden
This popular club-restaurant occupies a large courtyard within the harbour's nightlife district. It offers a decent choice of Turkish and international food, and later plays pop, dance and the odd Turkish tune to a riotous crowd. ◈ *Müftüler Cad, Demirciler Sok 99 • Map L5 • (0242) 511 15 82 • €€€€*

6 Eski Ev (The Old House)
A good place to sample authentic Turkish cuisine in reasonably authentic surroundings, Eski Ev occupies a restored house on one of Alanya's main shopping streets. ◈ *Damlataş Cad 44 • Map L5 • (0242) 511 60 54 • €€€*

7 Redtower Brewery
Situated in the lively harbour area, this busy place has a restaurant with an international menu and a roof terrace with a sushi bar. It also brews its own superb beer. ◈ *Iskele Cad 80 • Map L5 • (0242) 513 66 64 • Open year-round • €€€*

8 Willis Kneipe
Unsurprisingly popular with the town's numerous German visitors, Willis Kneipe is the place for Germanic delights such as *sauerkraut* and *bratwurst*. ◈ *Güzelyali Cad 30 • Map L5 • (0242) 512 25 79 • Open year-round • €€*

9 Oscar's Scandinavian Restaurant
Oscar is a characterful Turk who spent many years as a chef in Norway. This popular outdoor restaurant offers over 120 Norwegian dishes. ◈ *Sirinevler Sok 6 • Map L5 • (0242) 511 24 68 • €€€€*

10 Ravza
Set in the harbour district, Ravza serves freshly caught fish as well as local and international dishes. ◈ *Yeni Çarşı Zambak Sok, Ziraat Bankası Karşısı 13 • Map L5 • (0242) 513 39 83 • Open year-round • €€*

Restaurants are open between early April and late October unless otherwise stated.

Price Categories

For a three-course meal for one with half a bottle of wine (or equivalent meal), taxes and extra charges.

€	under €15
€€	€15–€25
€€€	€25–€30
€€€€	€30–€35
€€€€€	over €35

Moonlight, Side

🔟 Restaurants outside Alanya

1 Moonlight, Side
Occupying a lovely position on the tip of the peninsula, this stylish restaurant with a good wine list offers fish specialities such as swordfish. ◎ *Barbaros Cad 49 • Map K5 • (0242) 753 14 00 • €€€€*

2 Orfoz, Side
Orfoz provides great service in a stylish seaside setting. Fresh fish and seafood – including sea bass, lobster and shrimps – are delivered daily, and there's a good selection of Anatolian wines. ◎ *Liman Cad 58/B, Side • Map K5 • (0242) 753 13 62 • €€€€*

3 The End, Side
One of the many restaurants clustered beside the harbour, The End is literally at the end of the peninsula. Specialities include Alibaba Kebab, cooked in a stone oven; fresh fish; and some superb Anatolian boutique wines. ◎ *Liman Cad • Map K5 • (0242) 753 20 05 • €€€€*

4 Lighthouse Club, Side
This stylish club-restaurant with sea views in all directions serves excellent Italian cuisine in the evenings. ◎ *Liman Cad • Map K5 • (0242) 753 35 88 • €€€€*

5 Soundwaves, Side
Established in 1977, this quirky pirate-themed eatery offers a simple choice of Turkish dishes and pizza that can be enjoyed on a terrace overlooking the sea. ◎ *Barbaros Cad 16 • Map K5 • (0242) 753 10 59 • €€*

6 Şarapsa Han, Alanya
This atmospheric 13th-century inn provides an all-inclusive entertainment package; guests sample a variety of Turkish dishes before being treated to a spectacular dance show. ◎ *14 km (9 miles) west of Alanya • Map L5 • (0242) 565 00 20 • Closed Mon, Sat, Sun L • €€€€*

7 Aspendos Restaurant, Aspendos
Just outside the village of Belkis near Aspendos, this restaurant serves a mixed menu of Turkish and international food on a delightful outdoor terrace above the Köprü river. ◎ *Belkis Beldesi, Serik • Map J4 • (0242) 735 73 00 • €€*

8 Roman Restaurant, Belek
This well-run place offers a mainly European menu with a number of Turkish options. Live music at weekends. ◎ *Cumhuriyet Cad 8, Kadriye • Map J5 • (0242) 735 53 63 • Open year-round • €€€*

9 Ocakbaşı Restaurant, Manavgat
This is a lovely spot from which to watch boats cruise up and down the Manavgat river. Traditional Turkish menu. ◎ *Yittisar Mah, 7017 Sok 2, Eski Otogar • Map K5 • (0242) 746 44 95 • Open year-round • €€€*

10 La Pizza, Manavgat
La Pizza is an excellent chain serving a reliable range of pizzas, fast food and salads. ◎ *Lise Cad 31/A • Map K5 • (0242) 743 07 70 • Open year-round • €*

Left **Gate of Augustus, Ephesus** Right **Bodrum viewed from the castle**

Further Afield

While most visitors to southwest Turkey remain on the coast for the duration of their stay, some join day trips or rent cars to visit the region's inland attractions. It's certainly worth the effort to see the superb ruins at Ephesus, Hierapolis and Aphrodisias; the culture shock of conservative Konya is an experience to savour; and the Turkish Lake District offers visitors the waterside peace they may have found lacking at crowded seaside resorts. Travelling further west along the coast brings you to Bodrum, a popular destination of enormous charm; Kuşadası, a resort town catering to package tourists; and the great port of İzmir, whose thoroughly modern fabric has absorbing pockets of history woven into it.

View of Kuşadası

🔟 Sights

1. İzmir
2. Ephesus
3. Kuşadası
4. Priene
5. Didyma
6. Bodrum
7. Aphrodisias
8. Pamukkale and Hierapolis
9. Lake Eğirdir
10. Konya

Preceding pages **The eerily beautiful travertines of Pamukkale**

1 İzmir

Known in ancient times as Smyrna, and successively under Greek, Roman, Byzantine and Ottoman rule, İzmir was granted to Greece in 1919 under the Treaty of Sèvres – only to be wrested back by Turkish forces in 1922, at the end of the Greco-Turkish War *(see p34)*.

Konak Mosque, İzmir

Today, after Istanbul and Ankara, it is Turkey's third largest city, an urban sprawl of office buildings, flyovers and concrete apartment blocks. After the Greeks left in the population exchange of 1923 *(see p34)*, the Turks destroyed much of the old city, but several buildings have survived in the central district around Konak Square, including an ornate 19th-century clock tower, next to which nestles the tiny and exquisitely simple Konak Mosque. ✎ *Map A1*

2 Ephesus

Established by the ancient Greeks in the 10th century BC, Ephesus was already one of the coast's major settlements by the time the Romans gained control in 133 BC. Chosen as the capital of the Roman province of Asia, it grew to be second in importance only to Rome – a status reflected in the great temples and marble streets with which the city was furnished. St Paul and St John both preached in Ephesus, and are thought to have brought the Virgin Mary to live here in her later years *(see pp14–17)*.

3 Kuşadası

Kuşadası is probably the least characterful of the major Turkish resorts, but the town is still a hugely popular destination for package tourists and cruise ships. Although the Old Town consists of just a few narrow streets, much of the large central shopping area has been pedestrianized, and there's a wide choice of bars and restaurants. Nightlife is predictably wild; those in search of all-night partying are unlikely to be disappointed. ✎ *Map A2*

4 Priene

Occupying a dramatic spot beneath a rocky escarpment, Priene was established in the 4th century BC. It was among the first settlements to be laid out in a grid pattern, by the pioneering town planner Hippodamus (498–408 BC). The lack of Roman influence at Priene meant that, unlike most other settlements, its Hellenistic architecture remained largely untouched. Much of the site is overgrown, but visitors can see significant ruins including the Temple of Athena, the well-preserved theatre and the *bouleuterion*, where council meetings were held. ✎ *Map A3*
• *Open 8am–6pm daily* • *Adm*

Remains of the Temple of Athena, Priene

Ionian philosphy

The coastal region around ancient Smyrna (modern-day İzmir) was called Ionia and produced some of the world's earliest philosophers in the 6th century BC. The wise Ionians spent their days attempting to explain the nature of matter through abstract reasoning rather than experimentation. Leading lights included Diogenes of Apollonia and Heraclitus, who was also known as "the Weeping Philosopher".

5 Didyma

Even in ruins, Didyma's Temple of Apollo remains a magnificent sight. Built in the 6th century BC on a stepped platform, it was once surrounded by 120 marble columns. Worshippers would travel from all over Anatolia to hear the prophesies of the priest of Apollo. The sacred path they followed from the coast was lined with statues until 1858, when they were acquired by the British Museum. ✏ Map A3 • Open 8am–7pm daily • Adm

Head of Medusa at the Temple of Apollo, Didyma

6 Bodrum

The appealing whitewashed houses that pepper the hilly terrain around Bodrum are in striking contrast to the relentless rows of hotel blocks at the nearby resorts of Marmaris and Kuşadası; yet Bodrum attracts a similar number of tourists. The town has a 15th-century castle built by the crusading Knights Hospitaller, a delightful bazaar quarter packed with craft shops, bars and eateries and a thriving nightlife scene revolving around Halikarnas Disco – one of the coast's top clubs. ✏ Map A4

7 Aphrodisias

Positioned on a high plateau, Aphrodisias functioned as a shrine to Aphrodite, the goddess of love, centuries before the site became a thriving Roman settlement. It lay buried beneath the village of Geyre until the 1960s, when Turkish archaeologist Kenan Erim revealed the grand ruins of this extensive town. Among the highlights are the *tetrapylon*, a reconstructed temple; an exceptionally well-preserved Roman stadium; and the foundations of Aphrodisias' most important building, the Aphrodite temple, converted to a church in the 5th century. ✏ Map D3 • Open 8:30am–7pm daily • Adm

8 Pamukkale and Hierapolis

The sight of an entire hillside covered with a cascade of brilliant white travertines brimming with steaming spring water is certainly worth the three-hour coach journey from the coast. Besides paddling in Pamukkale's famous pools, visitors can explore the scattered ruins of the Roman city of Hierapolis, peruse fascinating exhibits in a Roman bathhouse and swim in the Antique Pool once used by the Romans. The site is best visited during the evening or early morning to avoid the crowds *(see pp18–19)*.

Ruins of theatre, Hierapolis

Lake Eğirdir

9 Lake Eğirdir

Although it's often used as a mere stopover between Konya and the coast, Eğirdir and the picturesque Turkish lakes region certainly warrant a longer visit. At 482 sq km (186 sq miles), Lake Eğirdir is the fourth largest lake in Turkey. At its southern end, Eğirdir town is a bustling little place connected by a narrow causeway to a pair of islands crowded with lakeside fish restaurants and *pensions*. Visitors can fish, go for boat trips or enjoy the mountainous surroundings that provide ample opportunities for hiking, mountain biking and jeep safaris. ◎ *Map J2*

10 Konya

Anyone arriving fresh from the coast in one of Turkey's most conservative towns may be in for a surprise, as many women here observe the Islamic dress code. Konya is geographically and culturally part of Central Anatolia, and although it's only 150 km (94 miles) from the coast, its ramshackle bazaars and Selçuk architecture are a world away. Once home to the Sufi mystic Mevlâna (1207–73), the town has been associated with whirling dervishes ever since and hosts an annual Mevlâna Festival *(see p39)* in December. ◎ *Map M2*

A 3-Day Inland Tour

Day 1

Start early from Marmaris and take the road north to **Muğla** (57 km/36 miles), with its Ottoman-era buildings *(see p110)*. From here head northeast towards Tavas (95 km/59 miles), where you'll see signs for **Aphrodisias** (39 km/24 miles). Linger in these atmospheric ruins and have a late lunch at one of the restaurants nearby. Return to Tavas and continue northeast until the E87 highway, which will take you the 47 km (29 miles) to Denizli, from where it's 25 km (16 miles) north to **Pamukkale**. Stay over at one of the town's family-run guest houses and visit the glistening white hillside travertines early next morning to beat the crowds.

Day 2

The ruins of **Hierapolis** lie beyond Pamukkale; allow at least a couple of hours to explore them. Have lunch at the **Antique Pool**'s busy eatery, or at one of the quieter restaurants in the village. **Ephesus** *(see pp14–15)* is a three-hour drive west (190 km/119 miles) along the E87; either arrive there late and sleep at neighbouring Selçuk, or set off from Pamukkale early the next morning.

Day 3

Two to three hours will suffice for the dramatic ruins of Ephesus. Follow this with a visit to the **Ephesus Museum in Selçuk** *(see pp16–17)*, where you can lunch at the welcoming **Amazon** restaurant *(see p113)*. From Selçuk, extend your trip to include **Didyma** and **Bodrum**, or return the 200 km (125 miles) to Marmaris.

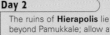

Around Turkey's Southwest Coast – Further Afield

Left **Güllük's harbour** Centre **The theatre at Miletus** Right **Ruined island monastery, Lake Bafa**

Best of the Rest

1 Muğla
A half-hour drive north from Marmaris, Muğla is an appealing provincial town with a number of restored Ottoman-era houses – a refreshing contrast to some over-developed coastal resorts. There's a good local museum. ◈ *Map C4*

2 Antioch ad Pisidiam
Frequently visited by St Paul in the 1st century AD, the ancient city of Antioch ad Pisidiam is now a fascinating archaeological site. ◈ *Map J1*
• Open 8am–5pm daily • Adm

3 Mount Davraz
Though there's not much of interest here during summer, during the winter months Mount Davraz is a small but busy ski resort, with over 6 km (4 miles) of runs for all levels. ◈ *Map H3*

4 Lake Bafa
Declared a national park in 1989, Lake Bafa is home to over 200 bird species as well as a large number of endemic plants. There are boat trips to the ruins of an island monastery, and plenty of opportunities for hiking and fishing. ◈ *Map B3*

5 Miletus
Though much of this once great Ionian city now lies beneath an overgrown expanse of marsh and mud, ruined structures such as the 15,000-seat theatre make a visit worthwhile. ◈ *Map A3*
• Open 8am–7pm daily • Adm

6 Iotape
Founded by the Seleucid King Antiochus IV (215–163 BC) and named after his wife, Iotape was once a small trading port. Jumbled ruins at the idyllic location include a triple arch that still stands today. ◈ *Map L6*

7 Lake Beyşehir
This 650-sq-km (251-sq-mile) expanse of water is part of the Turkish Lake District. Although tourism is less developed here than at Eğirdir *(see p109)*, there are opportunities for boating, walking and cycling. ◈ *Map E1*

8 Labranda
Set on a hillside high above a plain, this ancient sanctuary of Zeus is reached by a steep, winding road that few tourist buses attempt. Dating back to the 7th century BC, the temple ruins can still be seen. ◈ *Map B3*

9 Güllük
Particularly popular with British tourists, Güllük occupies a hillside above a small fishing harbour and several sheltered bays. There are very few large hotels here. ◈ *Map B4*

10 Trips to Greek Islands
Ferries go from Kuşadası to Samos (1hr 45 mins) twice a day in high season. Bodrum has daily ferry services to Kos (1 hr) and the Datça Peninsula (1hr 45 mins), and a hydrofoil to Rhodes (2hrs 15 mins). ◈ *Map A2, A4*

Ali Baba, Kuşadası

🔟 Restaurants in Kuşadası & Bodrum

1 Tuti, Bodrum
Part of the 5-star Marmara Hotel *(see p126)*, Tuti affords spectacular views of Bodrum from its hilltop terrace. An inventive menu combines Turkish and Western cuisine, impeccably served. 🕲 *Yokusbaşi Mah, Sulu Hasan Cad • Map A4 • (0252) 313 81 30 • €€€€€*

2 Planet Yucca, Kuşadası
Planet Yucca has something for everyone – the menu lists Chinese, Indian, Italian, Mexican and Turkish options – and attracts a merry crowd of foreign tourists. Entertainment includes karaoke and an Elvis impersonator. 🕲 *Saglik Cad 65 • Map A2 • (0256) 612 07 69 • €€*

3 Kazim Usta, Kuşadası
On the harbour's edge, Kazim Usta has been open for over 60 years and serves a reliable range of Turkish and international dishes. 🕲 *Liman Cad 16 • Map A2 • (0256) 614 12 26 • Open year-round • €€*

4 Ali Baba, Kuşadası
Ali Baba offers excellent seafood, a wide range of freshly prepared meze and a good choice of Turkish wines. 🕲 *Belediye Turistik Çarşisi 5 • Map A2 • (0256) 614 15 51 • Open year-round • €€*

5 Rigolo, Kuşadası
Unlike many tourist-oriented restaurants, Rigolo provides diners with a relaxed ambience. Steak and roast beef feature on the menu. 🕲 *Atatürk Bulvari 42 • Map A2 • (0256) 618 12 13 • €€*

6 Gemibaşi, Bodrum
Set right on the seafront, this well-established restaurant serves Turkish staples. 🕲 *Neyzen Tevfik Cad 176 • Map A4 • (0252) 316 12 20 • Open year-round • €€*

7 La Jolla Bistro, Bodrum
This popular restaurant has succulent steaks, an impressive selection of sushi and a superb cellar of Turkish and international wines. 🕲 *Neyzen Tevfik Cad 174 • Map A4 • (0252) 313 76 60 • €€€€*

8 Avlu, Kuşadası
Tucked away down a bustling backstreet in the bazaar quarter, Avlu serves a range of good-value Turkish dishes. 🕲 *Cephane Sok 15 • Map A2 • (0256) 614 79 95 • €*

9 Marina Yacht Club, Bodrum
An excellent choice of Turkish and international cuisine is served in this smart restaurant with a lovely roof terrace overlooking the marina. T-bone steaks are a speciality. 🕲 *Neyzen Tevfik Cad 5 • Map A4 • (0252) 316 12 28 • €€€*

10 Club Caravanserail, Kuşadası
Worth visiting for the interior alone, this hugely atmospheric restaurant occupies a 17th-century *kervansaray* (inn), where shaded tables fill the large courtyard. The menu features a wide selection of Turkish and international cuisine. 🕲 *Atatürk Bulvari 2 • Map A2 • (0256) 614 41 15 • €€€€€*

 Restaurants are open between early April and late October unless otherwise stated.

Left **Alibaba Carpets, Turgutreis** Centre **Bodrum Bazaar** Right **Grand Bazaar, Kuşadası**

🔟 Shops and Markets

1 Bodrum Bazaar
Bodrum's bazaar is a joy to explore. Packed into a maze of characterful whitewashed houses overhung with ivy, its shops offer everything from colourful spices to sparkling jewels. ✆ *Map A4*

2 Grand Bazaar, Kuşadası
A jumbled assortment of shops, cafés, bars and restaurants flanking the Old Town's cobbled streets, the Grand Bazaar is by far Kuşadası's most appealing quarter. ✆ *Map A2*

3 Alibaba Carpets, Turgutreis
Set in a small seaside resort 20 km (13 miles) east of Bodrum, this well-established shop has an excellent selection of carpets that can be shipped direct to your home. ✆ *Yakamoz 3 Sok • Map A4*

4 Bazaar 1001, Kuşadası
Bazaar 1001 is an atmospheric carpet shop located in a 200-year-old house in Kuşadası's Grand Bazaar. Beautiful rugs from all over Turkey adorn the walls; many more await inspection, stacked up in piles. Home delivery service is available. ✆ *Cephane Sok 20 • Map A2*

5 Engin Dalyancı, Bodrum
Known as "the Fish Painter", Engin Dalyancı is a successful local artist whose brightly coloured souvenir artworks are eagerly snapped up by tourists at his shop in Bodrum's bazaar. ✆ *Cumhuriyet Cad 55 • Map A4*

6 Odeon Shopping Centre, Bodrum
Dotted with palm trees, cacti and water features, this modern mall on the outskirts of town has indoor and outdoor shopping zones, children's play areas and a five-screen cinema. ✆ *Emin Anter Bulvari, Kibris Sehitleri Cad • Map A4*

7 Marina Shopping Boutique, Bodrum
This pleasant, palm-shaded arcade of upmarket cafés and tastefully styled boutiques beside Bodrum Marina carries well-known brands like Tommy Hilfiger and Ralph Lauren. ✆ *Neyzen Tevfik Cad • Map A4*

8 Kuşadası Market
In Kuşadası's vibrant, colourful market, traders from around the region sell their vegetables, dairy products and crafts. It's a wonderful place to sample the local culture. ✆ *Map A2 • Tue, Fri*

9 Scala Nuova, Kuşadası
This modern mall jutting out into the sea alongside Kuşadası's busy ferry terminal has global chains like Starbucks and KFC as well as smart souvenir and carpet shops. ✆ *Kuşadası Harbour • Map A2*

10 Naturel Leather, Kuşadası
With over 5,000 items in stock, Naturel Leather sells a wide range of good-quality men's and women's leather clothing and bags in a diverse assortment of colours and styles. ✆ *Liman Cad 1 • Map A2*

Price Categories

For a three-course meal for one with half a bottle of wine (or equivalent meal), taxes and extra charges.

€ under €15
€€ €15–€25
€€€ €25–€30
€€€€ €30–€35
€€€€€ over €35

Selene's, Lake Bafa

🔟 Restaurants

1 Mevlevi Sofrasi, Konya
This classy restaurant with a terrace facing Mevlana's tomb *(see p55)* serves a broad range of Turkish cuisine including a number of local specialities. ◈ *Aziziye Mah, Amil Çelebi Sok 1 • Map M2 • (0332) 353 33 41 • Open year-round • €€€*

2 1888, İzmir
Occupying the ground floor and courtyard of a characterful old building, 1888 is frequented by a 30-something crowd of young professionals. Italian and Mexican cuisine is served. ◈ *Cumhuriyet Blv 248, Alsancak • Map A1 • (0232) 421 66 90 • Open year-round • €€€*

3 Big Apple, Yeşilada, Eğirdir
Set on the western edge of one of two tiny islands connected to Eğirdir by a narrow causeway, Big Apple is known for its freshly caught fish – the grilled lake bass is excellent. ◈ *Atayolu Cad, Sok 1, Yeşilada • Map J2 • (0246) 311 45 55 • €€*

4 Amazon, Selçuk
At this welcoming place with outdoor tables squeezed onto a pavement beside the restaurant's vegetable garden, the amiable owner provides delicious, fresh Turkish cuisine. ◈ *Anton Kallinger Cad 22 • Map A2 • (0232) 892 38 79 • €€*

5 Selene's, Lake Bafa
Diners can sample a wide range of meze and fresh fish dishes on a delightful shaded terrace overlooking the lake. ◈ *Map B3 • (0252) 543 52 21 • €€*

6 Kemal'in Yeri, İzmir
Known for its great seafood, this smart restaurant with polite and efficient service justifies its high prices. ◈ *1453 Sok 20/A, Alsancak • Map A1 • (0232) 422 31 90 • Open year-round • €€€€€*

7 Beyaz Park, Beyşehir
Part of the Beyaz Park Hotel, this simple lakeside restaurant with a number of outdoor tables serves decent Turkish food. ◈ *Atatürk Cad 1, Köprübaşi • Map K3 • (0332) 512 38 65 • €€*

8 Gülbahçesi Konya Mutfaği, Konya
The setting is a tastefully restored Ottoman-era building; on the menu, a mouth-watering selection of traditional Anatolian dishes. There's also a great view of Mevlâna's tomb. ◈ *Mevlana Külliyesi Yani • Map M2 • (0332) 353 07 68 • €€*

9 Fuego Beach Club, Güllük
Turkish and international dishes are on the menu at this relaxed seaside spot just beyond the harbour. ◈ *Hermias Cad 28 • Map B4 • (0252) 522 36 10 • €€€*

10 Mimoza Fish Restaurant, Gümüşlük
This stylish seafront restaurant, popular with locals and visiting yachters, is located in the tiny village of Gümüşlük, some 20 km (13 miles) east of Bodrum. Fresh fish and colourful salads feature on the menu. ◈ *Yali Mekii 44/1 • Map A4 • (0252) 394 31 39 • €€€€*

Restaurants are open between early April and late October unless otherwise stated.

STREETSMART

TOP 10 OF TURKEY'S SOUTHWEST COAST

Left **UK passport** Right **Children playing in the sun**

Planning Your Trip

1 When to Go
The tourist season opens at the beginning of April and runs until the end of October, when many facilities close for the winter. Temperatures reach an average of 35°C (95°F) in high season – not surprisingly, this is when resorts are at full capacity. It's much quieter in September and October, with average temperatures around 26°C (79°F) and the sea still warm.

2 What to Pack
The Turkish coast gets swelteringly hot in July and August, so thin cotton clothing and a hat are essential. There's little likelihood of rain, but on cool evenings in April and October you may need a light sweater or jacket. Pharmacies are widespread, but travellers are still advised to carry adequate supplies of any medication they require.

3 Passports and Visas
Upon entry to Turkey, passports must be valid for at least six months. Citizens of the following countries require three-month multiple-entry tourist visas, purchased in cash at the point of entry: Australia, Austria, Ireland, Spain, UK and USA ($15); Canada (€45); South Africa (€10). Check the Turkish Ministry of Foreign Affairs website (www.mfa.gov.tr) for the latest information.

4 Customs Regulations
It is illegal to export antiquities – that is, cultural artifacts such as carpets, coins, icons, coloured tiles, ceramics, paintings and sculptures over 100 years old – without an export certificate from a Turkish museum. Turkey is very strict concerning drugs – sniffer dogs are used at most airports, and there are severe penalties for drug-smuggling.

5 Insurance
Although insurance is not obligatory for travel in Turkey, it is highly recommended that visitors take out comprehensive travel insurance prior to arrival. Travellers who bring their own vehicles into the country must have valid Green Card insurance, which can be purchased at the border.

6 Driving Licence
Anyone driving their own vehicle or renting a car in Turkey must carry a valid national driving licence. To rent scooters and motorbikes with engines over 50cc, a valid motorcycle licence is required.

7 Time Difference
Turkey is 2 hours ahead of both Greenwich Mean Time and British Summer Time; 6 hours ahead of New York; and 9 hours ahead of Los Angeles. Sydney is 7 hours ahead of Turkey.

8 Electrical Appliances
The Turkish power supply is 220–240 volts AC, and sockets take plugs with two round pins. Most appliances with two-pin European-style plugs will work in Turkish sockets. Appliances with standard UK three-pin plugs will need an adaptor. North American and Canadian 120-volt appliances require an adaptor and a step-down transformer.

9 Children's Needs
The intense heat of high season is the most likely problem to affect children used to cooler climates, so full sun protection is a must. Most towns have small parks with play areas, and the larger resorts usually offer children's clubs with organized activities. The majority of Turks love young children and will make them feel very welcome.

10 Vaccinations
No vaccinations are mandatory for travel to Turkey, but visitors should have a tetanus booster before their trip and consider having a hepatitis B vaccination. Travellers intending to visit areas off the beaten track, where sanitation may be poor, are advised to have vaccinations for hepatitis A and typhoid. There is little risk of malaria along the southwest coastline.
✎ *www.nathnac.org*

Left **Tour buses** Centre **Speed-limits sign** Right **Car-hire sign**

🔟 Getting There and Around

1 By Plane
While most tourists destined for Turkey's southwest coast travel via the major international airport at Antalya, the region has several other international airports further west – at Dalaman, Bodrum and İzmir. All of these serve European as well as some Middle-Eastern destinations, but flights to and from the USA and Australasia use the airports at Istanbul (Atatürk) or Ankara (Esenboğa).

2 By Sea
There are plenty of well-equipped marinas along the coastline *(see pp42–3)*, and a number of busy ferry ports. Bodrum has daily crossings to the Greek island of Kos; Marmaris and Fethiye have ferries and hydrofoil services to Rhodes; and ferries to Samos depart from Kuşadası.

3 By Car
The easiest way to reach Turkey from Europe by car is to take a car ferry from Brindisi to Çeşme via Igoumenitsa and Patras in Greece (31 hours); alternatively, from Venice to İzmir (63 hours). The other option is to travel overland to Istanbul, followed by a 10-hour drive to Antalya.

4 By Coach
Options for reaching Turkey from Europe by coach are rather limited; Eurolines don't currently offer a Turkish service. If, however, you are planning to travel to Turkey via Bulgaria or Greece, there are frequent buses to Istanbul from Sofia and Thessaloniki; then from Istanbul, comfortable air-conditioned coaches run to destinations all over the country.

5 Local Transport
Turkey has an extensive and generally reliable public-transport system. Large towns and cities are connected by regular coaches that often provide passengers with free cold drinks. *Dolmuşes* – minibuses seating up to 20 people – cover shorter distances between towns and villages.

6 Trains
There are regular international trains from Bulgaria and Greece to Istanbul; from there, you can travel by rail as far south as Selçuk, 20 km (13 miles) northeast of Kuşadası; and Burdur, 125 km (78 miles) north of Antalya – but no further.

7 Organized Excursions
Many of the attractions and historic sites along the coast are difficult to access without private transport, so package tourists tend to rely on organized excursions to visit the region. Most frequent during high season, trips range from a few hours to several days in duration, and generally include meals and accommodation.

8 Car Hire
Having your own vehicle is by far the best way to explore the coast's many attractions. Car-rental companies are ubiquitous, and usually offer quad bikes, scooters and off-road motorbikes, as well as cars of various sizes. Small Suzuki jeeps are a popular option for negotiating unpaved roads and sandy tracks.

9 Cycling
As long as you stick to the backroads and avoid the intense midday heat, cycling can be a pleasant way to travel in Turkey. Some of the resorts rent out bikes, but these are unlikely to be up to arduous trips, so serious cyclists should consider bringing their own. A few agencies run organized cycling tours of the coast, complete with back-up vehicle and guide *(see p123)*.

10 Travelling on Foot
There are plenty of walking and hiking opportunities along the coast. The Lycian Way *(see pp20–21)*. is an excellent starting point, and there are shorter marked trails in the region's various national parks. The minor roads connecting villages can also make good walking routes.

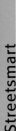

Streetsmart

Left **Official Turkish tourism website** Centre **Tourist Information Centre** Right **Turkish newspapers**

🔟 Sources of Information

1 Tourist Information Centres

The Turkish Ministry of Culture and Tourism has information centres at all the major resorts. Well stocked with colourful brochures, maps and leaflets, they are run by helpful multilingual staff.

2 Travel Agencies

Turkish travel agencies can be a great source of information. Their primary aim is to sign you up for a trip, but they are often willing to give detailed advice about travel in the region. Dragoman Travel in Kaş and Mevlana Tours in Antalya are particularly helpful. Ⓢ *Dragoman Travel Agency: Uzun Carsi Cad 15, Kaş; www.dragoman-turkey. com • Mevlana Tours: Tuzcular Mah, Paşa Camii Sok 5, Kaleiçi, Antalya; www.mevlanatour.com*

3 Consulates and Embassies

Britain has consulates in Antalya, Bodrum, Fethiye, Istanbul, Marmaris and İzmir; the USA has them in Adana, Istanbul and İzmir; Germany in İzmir, Antalya and Istanbul; Australia in Çanakkale and Istanbul; and New Zealand in Istanbul only. All national embassies are based in Ankara. Ⓢ *http://ukinturkey.fco. gov.uk • www.istanbul. usconsulates.gov • www. germanembassyank.com • www.turkey.embassy.gov. au • www.nzembassy.com*

4 Foreign-Language Bookshops

Most large Turkish bookshops in Alanya, Antalya and Marmaris have small English-language sections stocked with paperbacks, maps and travel-related titles. Museum shops are also a good source of foreign-language material on local sights and history.

5 Websites

There is a plethora of websites relating to travel in Turkey, and a great many of them are in English. Many of the main tourist centres have their own websites, and most hotels and some restaurants also maintain a site. The Turkish Ministry of Culture and Tourism has a helpful website. The UK Foreign Office and the US Department of State websites both offer up-to-date travel advice. Ⓢ *www.tourism turkey.org • www.fco.gov. uk • http://travel.state.gov*

6 Television

Although there are no dedicated English-language television channels in Turkey, many hotels subscribe to satellite or cable services with news and sports channels, such as BBC World, CNN, Euronews and Eurosport. In resorts like Marmaris, with a preponderance of English tourists, expect to see live UK television in bars and restaurants.

7 Local Newspapers

Today's Zaman and *Hürriyet* are Turkey's leading English-language newspapers. Both are excellent sources of local news. Printed editions are usually available in larger towns and resorts. Ⓢ *www.todayszaman.com • www.hurriyetdailynews.com*

8 Listings Magazines

None of the coastal resorts publish listings guides with details of upcoming events, but local tourist information centres will often be able to provide information about concerts, performances, exhibitions and festivals in the region.

9 Maps

Street maps can be found at tourist information centres and some hotels, but it's worth buying a more detailed map of the area before you leave home. Freytag & Berndt's two *Turkish Riviera* maps (1:150,000) are good for the coast. For hikers, there's an indispensible map in *The Lycian Way* by Kate Clow.

10 Private Guides

Licensed freelance tour guides for groups or individuals can be hired through local tourist information centres or travel agencies. Bookings should be made at least 24 hours in advance and prices range from 85 to 105 euros per day.

Left **Exchange Bureau sign** Centre **ATMs** Right **Turkish postal service logo**

🔟 Banking and Communications

1 Money

Turkey's currency is the Turkish Lira (TL), which subdivides into 100 kuruş. Banknotes come in six denominations: 5 TL, 10 TL, 20 TL, 50 TL, 100 TL and 200 TL. The Turkish Lira was previously known as the New Turkish Lira (YTL), which was introduced in 2005, knocking six zeros off Turkey's inflated former currency (called, rather confusingly, the Turkish Lira). The subsequent stability of the new currency led to the "New" being dropped in 2010; New Turkish Liras are no longer legal tender.

2 Banks

Banking hours are generally from 9am to 5pm on weekdays, with a one-hour closure for lunch between 12:30pm and 1:30pm. However, not all banks close for lunch, and some open on Saturdays. Most operate a ticket-based queuing system for customers.

3 Exchange Bureaux

Exchange bureaux (döviz para) provide the quickest and easiest way to change cash. They can be found in every tourist town and generally offer a decent rate of exchange. However, tourists should beware of unscrupulous bureaux that don't clearly advertise their exorbitant commission rates, which can sometimes be as high as 10 per cent.

4 Credit Cards

Credit and debit cards can be used for all kinds of purchases throughout Turkey. They are widely accepted in most of the larger supermarkets, hotels, restaurants and petrol stations, not to mention souvenir and carpet shops.

5 Postal Services

Post offices are branded with the insignia of the Turkish postal service, PTT. They open from 8am until midnight in larger towns; smaller branches open from 8am till 6pm. Letters and postcards sent from Turkey take a week or more to reach Europe and at least two weeks to reach the US or Australasia. Turkish post boxes are painted bright yellow.

6 Money Transfers

Western Union money transfers can be sent and received instantaneously in many of Turkey's banks and post offices. Bank-to-bank transfers take longer to process but usually incur a similar fee.

7 Internet Access

Internet cafés are widespread along the coast; your hotel or local tourist information centre will know the location of the nearest one. For anyone with a suitably equipped laptop, wireless (Wi-Fi) Internet is available at most restaurants, bars and cafés. Hotels usually provide Wi-Fi in their lobbies, but the signal is rarely strong enough to reach higher floors.

8 Mobile and Public Phones

Most mobile phones with roaming (but not those from North America) can be used in Turkey, or you can buy a pre-paid SIM card, which allows calls at local rates. To use a public telephone you need a telephone card; they can be purchased from post offices and street kiosks. Calls from hotel telephones are invariably very expensive.

9 Travellers' Cheques

Few high-street banks in Turkey will change travellers' cheques, and if they do, they are likely to charge a hefty commission – similar to the rate you will be charged in 4- and 5-star hotels. The best advice is to carry a debit card to withdraw cash from your bank account for a minimal fee.

10 ATMs

Cash machines are readily found in Turkish cities, but are few and far between in smaller settlements – so arm yourself with sufficient cash for any trips off the beaten track. To avoid the possibility of your card being blocked while you are abroad, notify your bank of your travel plans in advance.

Left **Sunburn** Centre **Mosquito repellents** Right **Pharmacy**

TOP 10 Security and Health

1 Emergency Services
Dial 155 for police, 112 for an ambulance and 110 for fire (177 for a forest fire). Ambulance response times are often quite slow, so if your condition is severe, call a taxi. For the coast guard, call 158; for tourism information, 170.

2 Crime
Turkey is generally considered a safe place to visit, with crime rates significantly lower than those of many European countries. However, petty crime is on the increase in tourist areas, and larger resorts have special "tourism police" who speak foreign languages.

3 Precautions
Taking a few simple precautions can reduce your risk of becoming the victim of petty crime: avoid unlit streets at night; always keep your bags in sight; carry cash and credit cards in a secure money belt; don't leave bags on view in vehicles; don't carry more cash than you need for the day; and lock up any valuables in the hotel safe.

4 Terrorism
Terrorism is a very real threat in Turkey, and although attacks are more frequent in the southeast of the country, coastal tourist resorts have been targeted in the past. Visitors are advised to remain vigilant and report any suspicious activities immediately. Security updates are posted on the travel pages of the UK Foreign Office and US Department of State websites (see p118).

5 Mosquitoes and Ticks
There's no danger of malaria on Turkey's southwest coast, but mosquitoes are a nuisance between dusk and dawn. Wear light, long-sleeved clothing and apply repellent to exposed skin. When walking in forests in Turkey, avoid ticks by using tick repellent and covering your arms and legs. Pharmacies sell tick-removing tools.

6 Sun and Sea Hazards
The summer sun is very strong in Turkey, so drink plenty of fluids to avoid dehydration and follow the usual precautions of slip, slop, slap (slip on a shirt, slop on sun cream, slap on a hat). Sharks have been known to approach beaches along the Mediterranean coast, but swimmers are more likely to have trouble with sea urchins and jellyfish.

7 Hospitals
Hospital standards in Turkey vary greatly, and tourists are generally advised to opt for private hospitals, which tend to be better equipped. Note that private hospitals will require proof of travel insurance. Consulates and tourist information centres can advise on the best local medical care.

8 Pharmacies
Pharmacies (eczane) are widespread; their symbol is a large red letter "E". Most of them open between 9am and 7pm from Monday to Saturday, but every district has a designated 24-hour pharmacy. Although most medicines are available or can be ordered, it's best to carry with you adequate supplies of any specific medication you require.

9 Dentists
Turkish dental care is generally of good quality, and significantly cheaper than in Europe. Tourist information centres and consulates should have a list of qualified English-speaking dentists. Note that travel insurance only covers emergency – not cosmetic – dental work.

10 Women Travellers
The best advice for women travellers in Turkey is to avoid prolonged eye contact with men, to ignore unwanted approaches and to take common-sense precautions such as not walking alone at night; requesting a masseuse (rather than a masseur) in mixed bathhouses; and so on. In tourist areas, Western-style clothes are completely acceptable.

If you are calling one of the emergency services from a mobile phone, add a zero before the number – e.g. 0155 for police.

Left **Antiques shop** Centre **Taxi** Right **Popular Turkish brand of bottled water**

TOP 10 Things to Avoid

1 Drugs
Turkey has strict anti-drug laws, and conviction for using, possessing or trafficking illegal drugs carries a heavy fine and a jail sentence of four to 24 years. Although outdated, the film *Midnight Express* is a powerful reminder of the consequences of drug trafficking in Turkey.

2 Buying Antiquities
It is illegal to export antiquities over 100 years old from Turkey – anyone convicted of doing so faces a prison sentence of up to 10 years. Many carpet shops will provide buyers with document-ation certifying that their carpets are not antiquities.

3 Taking Pictures in the Wrong Places
Never take photographs of military bases or installations, as doing so will leave you open to accusations of spying; if you are in any doubt about the nature of your subject, simply resist the photographic impulse and move on. It is considered polite to request permission from your subject before photo-graphing individuals.

4 Bag-Snatchers and Pickpockets
Pickpockets tend to operate in crowded areas like bus stations and markets, while bag-snatchers are on the lookout for any oppor-tunity. Keep your bags close by and in view at all times, and carry only as much cash as you need. Put a small amount in your wallet or purse and conceal the rest in a secure money belt.

5 Unscrupulous Taxi Drivers
Turkish taxi drivers are required by law to use digital taxi-meters. Avoid haggling over the fare and instead, insist that the driver starts the meter. Keep an eye on it, as there have been cases of a "magic button" being used by unscrupulous drivers to add 25 per cent or more to the bill at the end of the journey.

6 High-Season Heat
In July and August, at the height of the tourist season, temperatures along the coast average 36°C (97°F), and often rise above 40°C (104°F). If you want to avoid the heat – and save money – consider travelling during the cool, quiet months of April and May, or in September and October, when the sea still retains warmth from the summer.

7 Tap Water
Turkey's tap water is highly chlorinated, so it's advisable to drink bottled mineral water, which is readily available in a wide range of sizes. However, it is generally safe to have ice in drinks and to use tap water for brushing your teeth.

8 Marriage Proposals
Female travellers should be aware that some of the young Turkish men working in the tourist industry view the chance of marriage to a Wester-ner as a ticket to a better life, and may therefore be quick to propose. Such proposals are not to be taken lightly, so unless you're genuinely interested, try to avoid building false hopes.

9 Public Displays of Affection
While public displays of affection such as hugging and kissing are totally acceptable in the large tourist resorts along the southwest coast, where Western standards prevail, Turks generally frown upon such behaviour. Couples should exercise particular caution when visiting mosques, and in religiously conservative towns like Konya.

10 Prostitutes
It may seem surpris-ing, but prostitution has been legal in Turkey for many years, and there are municipal brothels with registered prostitutes who undergo regular health checks. However, the vast majority of sex-workers in Turkey – known as "Natashas", due to their by-and-large Russian origins – pose a potential health threat to clients as they are unreg-istered and unchecked.

Left **Kaş Camping, Kaş** Right **Fresh oranges on sale at Side market**

🔟 Budget Tips

1 Reduced Admissions
There's no universal policy regarding reduced admissions to museums and historical sites, but most have a single price for everyone over 12 years of age – children generally go free. A heavily discounted Museum Card was introduced some time ago, but this is currently available only to Turkish nationals.

2 Low Season
"Low season" is from April to early June and from mid-September to the end of October. It's a great time to avoid the crowds and the sweltering heat, and to take advantage of hotel and package-deal prices that are sometimes slashed by up to 50 per cent.

3 Camping
Many of the coast's camp sites *(see p130)* occupy idyllic seafront locations a good distance from crowded towns and resorts. Standards vary, but camp sites are generally decent, with clean bathrooms and washing facilities. Campers are charged per person and per tent; wooden bungalows are often available for a slightly higher rate.

4 Local Transport
It's certainly possible to rely on local transport to get around, but it takes patience, tenacity and a basic grasp of Turkish. *Dolmuşes* are numbered minibuses that run regular routes between towns and villages, and must be flagged down – the more remote your location, the less frequent the *dolmus*.

5 Walking and Biking
Cycling isn't popular among Turks, so if you decide to bike along the coast, be aware that local drivers are likely to ignore you. Walking is feasible, but there are relatively few dedicated footpaths, so that walkers must often trudge alongside main roads. The Lycian Way *(see p20–21)* is a far preferable alternative.

6 Eating Out
One of the cheapest ways to eat out in Turkey is to head for a canteen-style restaurant where locals order from a display of ready-prepared dishes. Quality is generally good as long as the place is busy – otherwise you may find that the food has been sitting there for rather too long.

7 Self-Catering
The self-catering options along the coast range from campsite bungalows through hotel rooms with small kitchens to rented apartments. Self-catering is an excellent way to save on the expense of daily trips to restaurants, and offers a great chance to shop in the local food markets for fresh produce.

8 All-Inclusive Packages
Many of the coast's mass-market hotels offer all-inclusive packages that cover drinks as well as meals and can be very good value. However, potential clients should take note that there have been many complaints of poor-quality food being the standard fare at such places. Check customer reviews before booking.

9 Markets
Markets are perfect for inexpensive snacks, pastries, fresh fruit and vegetables and sweets, as well as clothing and all sorts of other knick-knacks. They also provide a great opportunity for visitors to spend some time immersed in the local culture. Unlike in the bazaars, you won't usually be expected to haggle over the prices at local markets.

10 Student Travel
Student cards such as ISIC (International Student Identity Card) are less useful than they once were in Turkey, as nowadays many discounts are restricted to students who are Turkish nationals. There is no rail network along Turkey's southwest coast, and Eurolines bus passes don't extend to Turkey. Student-oriented travel agencies such as STA Travel arrange discounted flights and tours.
🌐 www.statravel.com

Left **Water sports off Uzunyalı Beach, Marmaris** Right **Walking the Lycian Way near Çıralı**

TOP 10 Specialist Holidays

1 Cultural
UK-based Journey Anatolia runs tours to introduce participants to the "real" Turkey by organizing visits to sites not usually seen by package tourists, and by offering accommodation at characterful hotels in unusual locations. Tour groups are kept small to minimize their impact on local communities and the environment. ✆ www.journeyanatolia.com

2 Health
Medical tourism is well established in Turkey, where many operations at its international-standard private hospitals cost around half of what their Western equivalents would charge. There are plenty of spa hotels (see p127) along the coast offering a wide range of treatments, and there's even a Dolphin Therapy Centre for the treatment of physical and learning disabilities. ✆ www.health-tourism.com

3 Walking
Middle Earth Travel runs one- and two-week Lycian Way walking trips, with accommodation at pensions and village houses along the way. British-based Inn Travel offers a more leisurely tour of the Lycian Way, with luxury accommodation at 3- and 4-star hotels. ✆ www.middle earthtravel.com • www.inntravel.co.uk

4 Cycling
Kaunos Tours in Dalyan run a reasonably-priced 8-day mountain-biking tour that includes the use of 24-gear bikes. The Dragoman Travel Agency in Kaş offers a similar package. ✆ www.kaunostours.com • www.dragoman-turkey.com

5 Water Sports
Water sports are the staple daytime entertainment along the coast. The greatest variety and most competitive prices can be found at Alanya, Kemer, Kuşadası and Marmaris. Options include banana boat rides, jet-skiing, parasailing and water-skiing.

6 Horse-Riding
Despite the delightful scenery and numerous mountain tracks, there are few trekking centres in the coastal region. Perma Ranch at Kaya Köyü is an established British-run centre that offers jumping tuition, day-trips and all-inclusive riding holidays. Activities Unlimited is based in Ölüdeniz (see p65).

7 Spas
Many of the larger hotels have spa centres offering the latest treatments. Facilities usually include a replica Turkish hamam (steam bath) with sauna, massage table and options such as aromatherapy, hot-stone massages, mudpacks and hydrotherapy.

8 Sailing
The coast has an abundance of marinas providing plenty of sailing opportunities for all levels. "Bareboat" packages allow qualified captains to charter boats for as long as they choose, while "flotilla" holidays involve several boats sailing independently but following a set itinerary and tour leader. Tour companies include Budget Sailing at Göçek and UK-based Nautilus Yachting. ✆ www.budget sailing.com • www.nautilus-yachting.com

9 Bird-watching
Birdwatch Turkey offers by far the most comprehensive bird-watching tours in different parts of the country, with experienced, enthusiastic guides. Tours include comfortable accommodation and local transport, range from one day to several weeks and can be tailored to fit groups' and individuals' needs. ✆ www.birdwatchturkey.com

10 Adventure
Based in Kaş, the Dragoman Travel Agency runs a number of different adventure-based holidays. Its packages include an 8-day option split between hiking, diving and sea-kayaking. Other activities include paragliding, coasteering, night snorkelling and gorge-walking (see p118).

Left **Smoking at an outdoor table** Right **Statue of Atatürk, the founder of modern Turkey**

Etiquette

1 Criticism of Turkey
Turks in general have a strong sense of nationalism and revere Atatürk, the founder of modern Turkey. They are unlikely to react favourably to criticisms either of him or of their country, and it is in fact illegal to show disrespect to Atatürk or to the Turkish flag, government or security services.

2 Appropriate Clothing
Turkey is a secular state, and many Turkish women dress in Western style; short skirts and skimpy tops are the norm in coastal towns with a high concentration of tourists. The conservative town of Konya is an exception; female travellers are advised to dress modestly there, as they would when visiting a mosque.

3 Hospitality
If you're invited out for a meal with Turks, it's the custom for the host to pay the bill. Don't try to split it as this is an alien concept; instead, invite your host for dinner another day. Avoid overordering; it's considered rude not to finish everything on your plate.

4 Meeting and Greeting
When meeting a group of Turks, start with the eldest and shake hands with everyone – men, women and children. Repeat the procedure when you leave. Try to master a few introductory greetings like *merhaba* ("hello"), *nasılsınız?* ("how are you?") and *memnum oldum* ("pleased to meet you") *(see pp142–3)*.

5 Islam
Although Turkey has been a proudly secular country since Atatürk's religious reforms in the 1920s, its Islamic heritage is many centuries old and Islam remains the dominant religion. Any criticisms or jokes aimed at Islam are very likely to cause offence.

6 Ramadan
Ramadan lasts for a month each year when devout Muslims abstain from eating, drinking and sexual relations between dawn and dusk. Although it has little impact on coastal tourist areas, visitors should be aware of the custom and avoid disrespectful behaviour such as shouting and drunkenness – especially near mosques.

7 Men and Women
In many Turkish towns and cities it's common to see couples kissing and cuddling in public and this certainly won't be a problem in tourist areas. However, it's advisable to be more circumspect when visiting mosques and conservative towns like Konya. Gay and lesbian travellers are unlikely to encounter problems, but overt displays of affection are best avoided.

8 Smoking
Around 65 per cent of the world's oriental tobacco is produced in Turkey, and despite the smoking ban in government offices, bars, cafés and restaurants that was introduced in 2008, the country still has a significant number of smokers. Despite the ban in restaurants, don't be surprised to see diners lighting up between and even during courses when eating at home or out of doors.

9 Pork and Alcohol
Very few restaurants in Turkey serve pork – with the exception of the British-oriented establishments along the coast, where you will be offered English breakfast made with imported bacon and sausages. Although it's frowned upon by devout Muslims, alcohol is widely available and consumed by many Turks.

10 Covering Your Head
It's only really necessary for women to cover their heads when entering mosques. If you don't have any headwear, mosque attendants will often be able to provide shawls or headscarves – alternatively, a handy tip is to wear a hooded top if you plan to visit a number of mosques.

Left **Viewing carpets, Kadıköy Carpet Co-op** Right **Turkish souvenirs, Grand Bazaar, Kuşadası**

🔟 Shopping Tips

Haggling
1 While there's no need to bargain in regular shops, haggling in the bazaars is a must if you want to avoid being fleeced. Expect to pay around half the initial asking-price for whatever it is that you've got your eye on, and don't make an offer unless you're sure you want to buy.

Opening Hours
2 During the holiday season, shops along the coast catering to the tourist market usually stay open till midnight or later, to compensate for slack trading in the midday heat. Shops in larger towns and cities generally open from 9am until 7 or 8pm.

Bargains
3 Unless you're a seasoned pro at haggling, it's unlikely that you'll net yourself a real bargain in the bazaars. That said, determined shoppers may well discover reasonably-priced Turkish souvenirs by comparing prices and stubbornly refusing to pay over the odds.

Carpets
4 Turkey is deservedly famous for its wonderful carpets with their broad range of patterns and colours. Sold all along the coast, they vary widely in price and quality, so it's certainly worth shopping around before making a purchase. Check rug patterns for consistency, and make sure that the colours aren't bleeding into one another.

Don't Rush
5 Don't be surprised if traders seem to be unpacking half the items in their shops in an attempt to secure your business, and be prepared to take a long time over the process of haggling. Turks are accustomed to spending hours over deals, punctuated by steaming glasses of sweet tea, so relax and enjoy the process.

Fakes
6 Turkey has a thriving trade in "fakes". The markets and bazaars of the southwest coast are a fake-shopper's paradise, whether the counterfeit items purport to be Rolex watches, Ray-Ban sunglasses or the ubiquitous Louis Vuitton bags; pretty much every popular brand of clothing and accessory has been copied. To the untrained eye there may seem little difference between the real thing and the copy, but remember: although they may seem like a steal, fakes are usually inferior both in quality of materials and in workmanship, and your "Rolex" may have a limited lifespan.

Antiques
7 Given Turkey's strict laws against the export of antiquities (see p121), tourists should exercise extreme caution when considering the purchase of anything that looks particularly ancient. Ensure that you see the paperwork certifying that the object is not an antique before going ahead with a purchase.

Refunds
8 Turkish legislation regarding refunds is thin on the ground, particularly when it comes to items purchased from bazaars and market stalls. Choose your goods carefully, and if you feel the need for a refund or exchange, you'll have to rely on the shopkeeper's goodwill.

Electronic Goods
9 Electronic goods in Turkey are generally more expensive than they are in Europe, so there's little point in purchasing them here. Anyone considering moving to Turkey with their possessions should bear in mind that their used electrical items will incur import taxes.

Duty-Free Allowances
10 Visitors can bring up to 200 cigarettes or 50 cigars into Turkey, and are permitted to purchase an additional 100 cigars and 400 cigarettes from a duty-free shop upon arrival. For alcohol, the limit is 5 litres (180 fl oz) of wine or spirits.

Left **Kismet Hotel, Kuşadası** Right **Mehmet Ali Ağa Mansion, Datça**

🔟 Luxury Hotels

1 Divan Antalya Talya Hotel, Antalya

This modern 5-star hotel boasts an enviable cliff-top position just south of the centre. The rooms are immaculate and guests have the use of an onsite *hamam*. 🚫 *Fevzi Çakmak Cad 30 • Map Q3 • (0242) 248 68 00 • www.divan.com.tr • €€€*

2 Marmara Hotel, Antalya

Among the innovative design features at this spectacular modern hotel are a 3-storey "revolving loft", which rotates slowly on its axis through a full 360°, and a lobby-cum-restaurant resembling a contemporary art gallery and fitted out with a giant swing. 🚫 *Eski Lara Yolu 136 • Map H5 • (0242) 249 36 00 • www.themarmara hotels.com • €€€*

3 Kempinski Hotel Barbaros Bay, Bodrum

Occupying a glorious position overlooking an unspoiled bay 14 km (9 miles) from Bodrum, the Kempinski oozes exclusivity. Guests have the option of helicopter or limousine transfer from nearby airports, and the lavish suites range from several hundred to over five thousand euros a night. 🚫 *Kızılağaç Köyü, Gerenkuyu Mevkii Yaliciftlik • Map A4 • (0252) 311 03 03 • www.kempinski-bodrum.com • €€€€€*

4 Arcadia, Çıralı

Arcadia's luxurious wooden bungalows, half-hidden by orange trees and palms, are scattered throughout the resort's attractive gardens, right beside the beach. 🚫 *Çıralı beachfront • Map H6 • (0242) 825 73 40 • www. arcadiaholiday.com • €€€€*

5 Mehmet Ali Ağa Mansion, Datça

In the 19th century, this magnificent mansion was home to the Governor of Rhodes. Its wonderfully atmospheric rooms have cedarwood floors and hand-decorated ceilings. 🚫 *Reşadiye Mah, Kavak Mevdanı • Map B5 • (0252) 712 92 57 • www.kocaev. com • €€€€€*

6 Swissotel Göcek Marina Resort, Göcek

This secluded, country-mansion-style hotel with its own private beach and marina occupies a sea-front spot in quiet Göcek. The sumptuous rooms have lovely sea and mountain views. 🚫 *Cumhuriyet Mah • Map D5 • (0252) 645 27 60 • www.gocek. swissotel.com • €€€€€*

7 Villa Mahal, Kalkan

Clinging to a clifftop high above the sea, this intimate Mediterranean-style hotel has 13 immaculate rooms with polished wooden floors, floor-to-ceiling windows and sea-view terraces. Guests can access a private swimming platform below. 🚫 *4 Sok, Kaş Kale Yolu • Map E6 • (0242) 844 32 68 • www. villamahal.com • €€€€€*

8 Kismet Hotel, Kuşadası

Set on a wooded peninsula above the marina, Kismet's somewhat regal interior has attracted royalty, including Queen Elizabeth II in 1971 and the King and Queen of Sweden in 2006. The palm-shaded garden is an ideal place to relax. 🚫 *Gazi Begendi Bulvari 1 • Map A2 • (0256) 618 12 90 • www.kismet.com.tr • €€€*

9 Golden Key Bördübet Hotel, Marmaris

Situated in a flawless location 20 km (13 miles) to the west of Marmaris on the forested slopes of Hisarönü Bay, this hotel's idyllic, flower-bedecked cottages are spread out in wonderful gardens beside a long sandy beach. 🚫 *Hisarönü Köyü, Bördübet Mevkii • Map C5 • (0252) 436 92 30 • www. goldenkeyhotels.com • €€€€*

10 Oyster Residence, Ölüdeniz

Set well apart from the hectic centre, this enchanting, traditionally-styled complex near the famous beach has gained a reputation for outstanding service. 🚫 *Belcekiz Mevkii, 1 Sok • Map E5 • (0252) 617 07 65 • www.oyster residences.com • €€€€*

Price Categories

For a standard, double room per night (with breakfast if included), taxes and extra charges.

€ under €50
€€ €50–€75
€€€ €75–€125
€€€€ €125–€200
€€€€€ over €200

Left **Ece Saray Marina & Resort, Fethiye**

🔟 Spa Hotels

1 Sheraton Voyager, Antalya

This enormous hotel has a full spa centre featuring a Turkish steam bath and Egyptian-themed Jacuzzis. A broad range of treatments is offered, including aromatherapy and hot-stone massage. ◈ *Sakip Sabanci Bulvari, Konyaalti Plaji • Map H5 • (0242) 249 49 49 • www.sheraton. com/antalya • €€€€€*

2 Vogue Hotel Avantgarde, Antalya

Situated between Antalya and Kemer, this stunning hotel offers a *hamam*, a snow-room and aromatic showers, along with many other pampering options. ◈ *Esentepe Mah, Ahu Ünal Aysal Cad 1 • Map H5 • (0242) 813 60 00 • www.avantgardevogue hotel.com • €€€€€*

3 Adam & Eve Hotel, Belek

This truly outstanding ultra-modern hotel has won numerous awards in recent years. A fantastic contemporary spa centre features multi-coloured lighting, industrial-inspired design and the very latest in spa technology. ◈ *İskele Mevkii • Map J5 • (0242) 710 14 00 • www.adam evehotels.com • €€€€€*

4 Ada Hotel, Bodrum

Tiny windows puncture the domed roofs of the Ada's superb *hamam*, and its circular bathing chambers are marble-clad in traditional style. The hotel itself is equally luxurious, with 19th-century Ottoman styling and tasteful antique furnishings. ◈ *Göl-Türkbükü Belediyesi, Bağarasi Mah PK 350• Map A4 • (0252) 377 59 15 • www.ada hotel.com • €€€€€*

5 Ece Saray Marina & Resort, Fethiye

Surrounded by immaculate gardens, this grand three-storey hotel has its own private harbour next to the marina. The well-equipped spa centre offers mineral baths and hydrotherapy jet massages, and there's a traditional *hamam*. ◈ *Karagözler Mevkii 1, Yat Limani • Map E5 • (0252) 612 50 05 • www.ecesaray.net • €€€€*

6 Hillside Beach Club, Fethiye

Set in a secluded bay, this exclusive, self-contained resort has a remarkable selection of spa facilities. It offers a wide range of Eastern therapies including warm-rice massage, body scrubs and body wraps using fruits and herbs. ◈ *Kalemya Köyü • Map E5 • (0252) 614 83 60 • www. hillsidebeachclub.com • €€€€€*

7 Kalkan Regency, Kalkan

Enjoy a traditional foam or scrub massage in the elegant Regency's marble-clad *hamam*. Seaweed and mudpack treatments are also available. The beauty centre offers haircuts, waxing and much besides. ◈ *Kalamar Yolu • Map E6 • (0242) 844 22 30 • www.kalkanregency. com.tr • €€€€€*

8 Hera Hotel, Kaş

Set on a wooded hillside near Kaş, the imposing-looking Hera offers a *hamam*, Jacuzzis, a sauna and a fitness centre. There's no beach, but swimming platforms have been cut into the rocks below. ◈ *Küçükçakil Mevkii • Map F6 • (0242) 836 30 62 • www. herahotel.com.tr • €€*

9 Club Belcekiz Beach, Ölüdeniz

This big 5-star resort right next to Ölüdeniz's famous stretch of beach offers two large pools, a capacious *hamam* and a wide range of spa treatments. ◈ *Corner of 227/229 Sok, Denizpark Cad • Map E5 • (0252) 617 00 77 • www. belcekiz.com • €€€€*

10 Aspawa, Pamukkale

Though it's nowhere near the standard of high-end spa hotels, the Aspawa does boast an outdoor pool with a constant flow of thermal water direct from the Pamukkale springs that are just a short walk away. The rooms are spotless. ◈ *Turgut Ozal 28 • Map E2 • (0258) 272 20 94 • www. aspawapension.com • €*

Left **Mehtap Pansiyon, Kaleköy** Right **Rosarium Hotel, Kemer**

🔟 Mid-Range Hotels

1 Miray Hotel, Alanya

One of the many mid-range hotels within sight of Cleopatra Beach, the Miray is a towering six-storey building with a restaurant perched on top. The rooms are kept clean, have partial sea views, and service is generally good. ✎ *Saray Mah, Atatürk Cad 146 • Map L6 • (0242) 512 95 50 • www.mirayotel.com • €€€*

2 Atelya Art Hotel, Antalya

One of the hidden gems of Antalya's Old Town, the Atelya occupies a restored 18th-century Ottoman house with original wooden floors and ceilings, period furniture and antique artworks. The rooms are spacious, and breakfast is served in a secluded garden. ✎ *Civelek Sok 21, Kaleiçi • Map P2 • (0242) 241 64 16 • www.atelya hotel.com • €*

3 Özge Hotel Bungalow, Çıralı

Just a couple of minutes' walk from the beach, the Özge is run by a friendly Turkish couple who prepare a buffet of mouthwatering local dishes every evening. The smart bungalows are spaced well apart and have a living area, an *en suite* bathroom and air conditioning. ✎ *Ulupinar Köyü • Map H6 • (0242) 825 73 17 • www. ozgebungalow.com • €€*

4 Happy Caretta Hotel, Dalyan

Set in mature, well-tended gardens, this lovely hotel with excellent service offers comfortable accommodation in cool, simple rooms with rustic furniture and tiled floors. Meals are served on a tree-shaded terrace by the edge of the river. ✎ *Maraş Cad, Kaunos Sok 26 • Map D5 • (0252) 284 21 09 • www. happycaretta.com • €€€*

5 Mehtap Pansiyon, Kaleköy

A short boat-ride from Üçağiz, this small hotel sits on the hillside at Kaleköy, a tiny village facing Kekova Island. It offers tranquillity and seclusion along with splendid views and whirlpool baths in every room. There's also space for camping. ✎ *Map F6 • (0242) 874 21 46 • www. mehtappansiyon.com • €€*

6 Gardenia Hotel, Kaş

An easy walk from the centre and little more than a stone's throw from the beach, the Gardenia occupies a hillside position with glorious views of the bay. It is tastefully furnished throughout and about half of the rooms have sea views; the large junior suite has its own private terrace. ✎ *Hükümet Cad 41, Küçükçakil Mevkii • Map F6 • (0242) 836 23 68 • www.gardeniahotel-kas.com • €€€*

7 Hideaway Hotel, Kaş

This appealing hotel has a great rooftop terrace where guests can enjoy excellent local cuisine. All rooms have balconies, and there's a swimming pool – though the sea is a short walk away. ✎ *Eski Kilise Arkasi 7 • Map F6 • (0242) 836 18 87 • www. hotelhideaway.com • €€*

8 Rosarium Hotel, Kemer

Just beyond the centre and within walking distance of the beach, this well-presented hotel set in private gardens has a play-area for children as well as small and large pools. ✎ *Rosarium Hotel, Atatürk Cad 4 • Map H5 • (0242) 814 50 36 • www. rosariumhotel.com • €€€*

9 Royal Maris Hotel, Marmaris

This good-value 4-star hotel has an excellent central seafront location. Facilities include fitness centre, Turkish bath and rooftop swimming pool. ✎ *Atatürk Cad 34 • Map N5 • (0252) 412 83 83 • www. royalmarishotel.com • €€€*

10 Oba Motel, Ölüdeniz

Set in lush gardens close to the beach, Oba's seven wooden bungalows are spacious and clean, with *en suite* bathrooms and air conditioning. ✎ *Belcekız Mevkii • Map E5 • (0252) 617 01 58 • www.obamotel. com.tr • €€€*

Price Categories

For a standard, double room per night (with breakfast if included), taxes and extra charges.

€ under €50
€€ €50–€75
€€€ €75–€125
€€€€ €125–€200
€€€€€ over €200

Kadir's Tree Houses, Olympos

Budget Stays

1 Ninova Pansiyon, Antalya

The rooms at this charming hotel tucked away down a narrow street are on the small side, but they're comfortable and clean, and there's a pretty walled garden to relax in. ✆ *Hamit Efendi Sok 9, Kaleiçi • Map P2 • (0242) 248 61 14 • €*

2 Sabah Pansiyon, Antalya

A popular backpackers' choice in Antalya's Old Town, this family-run pension offers spotless four-bed dorms as well as private rooms. There's a half-board option with delicious home cooking. ✆ *Kilincaslan Mah, Hesapci Sok 60 • Map P3 • (0242) 247 53 47 • www.sabah pansiyon.com • €*

3 Bodrum Backpackers, Bodrum

This well-established and very sociable hostel with friendly staff has private rooms and mixed dorms with *en suite* bathrooms, as well as a "cheap sleep" roof terrace. It's central and has Wi-Fi. ✆ *Atatürk Cad 37/B • Map A4 • (0252) 313 27 62 • www.bodrum backpackers.net • €*

4 Ferah Pension, Fethiye

This cosy pension offers neat private rooms and dorms, with bathrooms and air conditioning. The location is fairly central and the owners offer free pick-up from the bus station. ✆ *2 Karagözler Orta Yol 23 • Map E5 • (0252) 614 28 16 • www.ferahpension.com • €*

5 Villa Rhapsody, Kaya Köyü

The delicious home cooking at this friendly family-run hotel is reason enough to stay. Built in traditional style with large gardens and a pool, its immaculate rooms are furnished in modern style. The owners will arrange trips throughout the region. ✆ *Map E5 • (0252) 618 00 42 • www.villarhapsody.com • €*

6 Ekin Hotel, Kuşadası

Situated right beside Ladies Beach, the Ekin offers decent accommodation at very reasonable prices, and has its own section of beach. Buses and taxis can be used to reach the centre, 3 km (2 miles) north. ✆ *Kadinlar Denizi Cad 75 • Map A2 • (0256) 614 39 70 • www.kusadasiekinhotel.com • €*

7 Maltepe Pansiyon, Marmaris

An excellent budget option, this small, centrally located, family-run hotel has clean rooms with two, three or four beds and *en suite* bathrooms. Guests have the use of kitchen facilities and there are pretty gardens to front and rear. ✆ *Kemeralti Mah 66, Sok 9 • Map N5 • (0252) 412 16 29 • www.maltepepansiyon.com • €*

8 Kadir's Tree Houses, Olympos

Rebuilt after a serious fire in 2005, most of the tree-houses at this legendary complex have been replaced by rickety two-storey wooden cabins. If this is not for you, accommodation can also be had in bungalows and dorms, or on the neighbouring field (bring your own tent). ✆ *Kadir's Yörük Top Tree House • Map H6 • (0242) 892 12 50 • www.kadirstreehouses.com • €*

9 St. Nicholas Pension, Patara

The perfect place from which to explore Patara's beach and ruins, this homely pension has a choice of 11 clean rooms (six triple, five double) with *en suite* bathrooms and air conditioning. Meals are served in a large vine-shaded garden beside the swimming pool. ✆ *St Nicholas Pension No 100 • Map E6 • (0242) 843 51 54 • www.stnicholas pensionpatara.com • €*

10 Yukser Pansiyon, Side

This small pension has an ideal location in the heart of Side's old town, just a few minutes' walk from the beaches. The air-conditioned rooms come with TV and *en suite* bathrooms, and breakfast is served in a shady garden. ✆ *Sümbül Sok 4, Side • Map K5 • (0242) 753 20 10 • www.yukser-pansiyon.com • €*

Left **Kaş Camping** Right **Saklıkent Gorge Camp**

🔟 Camp Sites

1 Çıralı Camping
This large, tree-shaded camp site just a short walk from Çıralı Beach *(see p40)* is clean and well maintained. Toilet and shower facilities are adequate, and there's a large communal fridge. ✎ *Çıralı Beachfront • Map H6 • (0242) 825 71 86 • www.ciralicamping.com • €*

2 Aktur Camping, Datça
This exceptionally well-run site is unusually situated on the neck of a tiny spit of land jutting out from the Datça Peninsula *(see p69)*. Its first-class facilities include a communal kitchen area for campers. There's also a pleasant beachfront restaurant. ✎ *Aktur Village, Datça Peninsula • Map B5 • (0252) 724 68 36 • www.akturcamping.com • €*

3 Çubucak Camping, Datça
Çubucak's forested location at the beginning of the Datça Peninsula provides complete shade for campers. For a little extra you can pitch right by the pebble beach. ✎ *Datça Yolu 23 km, Jandarma Karakolu Yanı, Marmaris • Map C5 • (0252) 467 02 21 • www.cubucak camping.com • €*

4 Kabak Natural Life, Fethiye
Around 30 km (19 miles) south of Fethiye beside a secluded bay, this site features tree houses on rickety wooden stilts scattered across a rocky hillside; it also caters to campers. The price includes a lovely breakfast and Turkish buffet dinner. ✎ *Kabak Mah, Faralya Köyü • Map E5 • (0252) 642 11 85 • www.kabaknaturallife.com • €€*

5 Kaş Camping
Set amidst olive trees on a hillside just beyond Kaş's amphitheatre, this well-established camp site has rocky swimming platforms and a lovely beach bar and restaurant. It is also home to a diving school, Sundiving. ✎ *Hastane Cad 3, Kaş • Map F6 • (0242) 836 10 50 • www.kaskamping.com; sundiving.com • €*

6 Önder Camping, Kuşadası
Centrally located next to Kuşadası's marina, this well-arranged site features simple chalets, plenty of tree-shaded pitches for tents and caravans, a swimming pool, adequate washing facilities and an excellent restaurant. ✎ *Atatürk Bulvari 4, Sok 10 • Map A2 • (0256) 618 16 90 • www.onderotel.com • €*

7 Sugar Beach Club, Ölüdeniz
Sugar Beach faces the tranquil lagoon to the rear of Ölüdeniz beach. Popular with Turkish youngsters, this site has excellent facilities and colourful decor. Those without tents can opt for a comfortable wooden bungalow. ✎ *Ölüdeniz Cad 20 • Map E5 • (0252) 617 00 48 • www.thesugar beachclub.com • €*

8 Hotel Dört Mevsim, Pamukkale
Although it's more hotel than camp site, this small, family-run establishment in Pamukkale is happy to let campers pitch in its garden. It has toilet and shower facilities, a restaurant and a pool with thermal spring water. ✎ *Map E2 • (0258) 272 20 09 • www.hoteldort mevsim.com • €*

9 Saklıkent Gorge Camp
This fun camp site by the river organizes rafting, trekking, paragliding and canyoning. Guests can choose between tree houses, guest rooms and camping. Facilities include a riverside restaurant and a swimming pool. ✎ *Map E5 • (0252) 659 00 74 • www.saklikentgorge.com • €*

10 Sundance Nature Village, Tekirova
Perfect for anyone in search of a seaside retreat, this secluded site has its own private beach, a horse-riding centre and wooden chalets amongst the trees. A small grassy area is set aside for camping. Breakfast is included. ✎ *Map H6 • (0242) 821 41 65 • www.sundancecamp.com • €*

Cornelia De Luxe Resort, Belek

Price Categories

For a standard, double room per night (with breakfast if included), taxes and extra charges.

€	under €50
€€	€50–€75
€€€	€75–€125
€€€€	€125–€200
€€€€€	over €200

🔟 Resort Hotels

1 Lara Beach Hotel, Antalya

Set on Lara Beach just outside Antalya, the main selling-point of this smart modern resort hotel is its large seaside swimming pool and waterslide complex. ⬡ Kemerağzi Mevkii, Kundu Bölgesi • Map J5 • (0242) 352 31 31 • www.hotellarabeach.com • €€€€

2 WOW Kremlin Palace, Antalya

This spectacular resort, predictably popular with Russian tourists, has full-size replicas of a number of Moscow buildings, including St Basil's Cathedral and various Kremlin palaces. ⬡ Kundu Köyü, Lara • Map J5 • (0242) 431 24 00 • www.wowhotels.com • €€€€€

3 Cornelia De Luxe Resort, Belek

This superb seaside resort boasts a 27-hole golf course designed by champion golfer Nick Faldo. Guests have the choice of five excellent restaurants as well as all manner of sporting and leisure activities. ⬡ Ileribaşi Mevkii • Map J5 • (0242) 710 15 00 • www.corneliaresort.com • €€€€€

4 Susesi Hotel, Belek

Swimming pools meander their way through a large part of this hugely luxurious seaside resort. Several buildings have their own private outdoor pools for the king suites

on each floor. The prices are appropriately high. ⬡ Iskele Mevkii • Map J5 • (0242) 710 24 00 • www.susesihotel.com • €€€€€

5 Xanadu Resort Hotel, Belek

Xanadu's plush facilities include a large Roman amphitheatre that hosts live entertainment every evening. There are plenty of daytime activities too. ⬡ Acısu Mevkii PK 49 • Map J5 • (0242) 710 00 00 • www.xanaduresort.com.tr • €€€€€

6 Hapimag Sea Garden Resort, Bodrum

This huge resort occupies a forested hillside beside an idyllic private bay. Facilities include a replica of a Bodrum shopping street, a Turkish hamam, all kinds of water sports and nightly shows with live music and dance. ⬡ PK 3, Yalıçiftlik • Map A4 • (0252) 311 12 80 • www.hapimag-seagarden.com • €€€€€

7 Letoonia Club Hotel, Fethiye

Extending over an entire peninsula, this vast resort has 2 km (1.25 miles) of flawless beach. Guests are accommodated in hundreds of luxuriously appointed bungalows. The deal includes free entertainment for 4–16-year-olds. ⬡ Pacariz Burnu Mevkii • Map E5 • (0252) 614 49 66 • www.letoonia resorts.com • €€€€€

8 İncekum Beach Resort

In an ideal world this resort would be a little further from the main Antalya-to-Alanya highway, but it has plenty of attractive features, including an appealing central pool and a palm-shaded private beach beyond. Standards are high and service is excellent. ⬡ Map K5 • (0242) 532 17 17 • www.incekumbeach resort.com • €€€€€

9 The Maxim Resort Hotel, Kemer

Within walking distance of Kemer, the Maxim offers luxurious accommodation and high-quality facilities at a relatively affordable price, although few of the rooms have sea views. It has a short stretch of private beach, a spa centre and several swimming pools, and there are plenty of activities to keep the kids entertained. ⬡ Atatürk Bulvan • Map H5 • (0242) 814 70 00 • www.the maximhotels.com • €€€€

10 Club Ali Bey, Manavgat

By accommodating its guests in a grid of unobtrusive two-floor blocks, this pleasant resort has created the atmosphere of a laid-back holiday village. There's a water park, and a short section of private beach. ⬡ Kizilağaç Turizm Bölgesi • Map K5 • (0242) 748 73 73 • www.alibey.com • €€€€

Most of the resorts listed offer all-inclusive packages.

Left **Aqua Fantasy Holiday Village, Kuşadası** Right **Su Hotel, Bodrum**

Family-Friendly Hotels

1 Su Hotel, Bodrum

Bursting with character, this lovely hotel is a great choice for those in search of a secluded base close to Bodrum's centre. Larger rooms have sofa beds to accommodate children. ✆ *Tugutreis Cad 1201 • Map A4 • (0252) 316 69 06 • www.bodrum suhotel.com • €€€*

2 Azur Hotel, Çıralı

With rabbits, chicken coops, hammocks and a children's playground amidst trees and lush lawns, this bungalow complex near to Çıralı beach is ideal for families with kids. ✆ *Ulupınar Köyü, Çıralı • Map H6 • (0242) 825 70 72 • www. azurhotelcirali.com • €€€*

3 Assyrian Hotel, Dalyan

Guests can opt for family-sized self-catering apartments or cosy rooms in the hotel's bungalows. The complex has a large central pool, a children's play area and a private jetty, from which it's a 15-minute boat trip to the famous İztüzü Beach. ✆ *Map D5 • (0252) 284 32 32 • www.asurotel.com • €€€*

4 Manzara Villas, Dalyan

Run by a British travel agency, Manzara comprises a number of smart self-catering villas for between two and 18 guests. Each group of villas shares a swimming pool, a kid's pool, a self-service bar and a barbecue area. Some rooms have open fires for chilly autumn nights. ✆ *Map D5 • (01304) 375093 (UK) • www.manzara.co.uk • €€€*

5 Aquapark Hotel, Kaş

This modern hotel is ideal for families, with a huge seafront swimming pool, water slides and plenty of organized activities for kids. The rooms are bright and spacious, with balconies and great sea views. ✆ *Çukurbağ Yarımadası • Map F6 • (0242) 836 19 02 • www.aquapark.org • €€€*

6 Aquarius Hotel, Kaş

Situated 5 km (3 miles) from Kaş on the Çukurbağ peninsula, this pleasant hotel offers spacious family rooms in tastefully furnished buildings set around the hotel pool. There's a lovely seafront restaurant and a private paved "beach" area built onto the rocky shore. ✆ *Çukurbağ Yarımadası • Map F6 • (0242) 836 18 96 • www.aquariusotel.com • €€€*

7 Alatimya Village Hotel, Kemer

This large hotel offers all-inclusive packages to a high standard. Facilities include indoor and outdoor pools, tennis courts and a spa centre. There's a full range of entertainment for grown-ups and children. ✆ *Atatürk Cad • Map H5 • (0242) 814 69 00 • www. alatimya.com.tr • €€€€*

8 Aqua Fantasy Holiday Village, Kuşadası

Built around a massive aqua park, this 5-star complex has all manner of water-based entertainments. The hotel offers all-inclusive packages, along with a fully-equipped spa centre and daycare for younger children. ✆ *Ephesus Beach, Pamucak, Selçuk • Map A2 • (0232) 893 11 11 • www. aquafantasy.com • €€€*

9 Club Lykia World, Ölüdeniz

This appealing complex of unobtrusive buildings surrounded by trees and gardens occupies a prominent seafront position beyond the main resort area. Accommodation is in large rooms or spacious family apartments. Entertainment is laid on for both children and adults. ✆ *Kidrak Mevkii • Map E5 • (0252) 617 03 00 • www. lykiaworld.com • €€€€*

10 Ephesus Princess, Selçuk

The Ephesus Princess is an all-inclusive complex with a non-stop ice-cream bar for kids, as well as a playground, a cinema and a gaming area. Baby-sitting services are also available. Entertainers run daily kids' clubs. Rooms are smart and comfortable, and most have lovely sea views. ✆ *Pamucak Mevkii • Map B2 • (0232) 893 10 11 • www.princess.com.tr • €€€*

Kibala Hotel, Çıralı

Price Categories

For a standard, double room per night (with breakfast if included), taxes and extra charges.	€	under €50
	€€	€50–€75
	€€€	€75–€125
	€€€€	€125–€200
	€€€€€	over €200

Hotels with a Difference

1 Bedesten Hotel, Alanya

Set on a hillside, Alanya's most appealing hotel occupies a 13th-century building with thick walls and tiny windows. There's a pleasant garden and the terrace has wonderful views. ⚲ İç Kale • Map L5 • (0242) 512 12 34 • €€€

2 Tekeli Konakları, Antalya

This attractive hotel in Antalya's atmospheric old town consists of six superbly renovated Ottoman-era houses set around a leafy courtyard, with swimming pool and restaurant. The rooms have traditional-style furnishings and modern touches such as Wi-Fi. ⚲ Dizdar Hasan Sok, Kaleiçi • Map N2 • (0242) 244 54 65 • www.tekeli.com.tr • €€€

3 Tuvana Hotel, Antalya

This splendid hotel artfully integrates modern facilities in a traditional architectural setting; the original structure was built in the 18th century for an Ottoman dignitary. ⚲ Tuzcular Mah, Karanlık Sok 18, Kaleiçi • Map P2 • (0242) 247 60 15 • www.tuvanahotel.com • €€€

4 Kibala Hotel, Çıralı

The Kibala comprises spacious wooden bungalows set well apart in lush gardens, just a short walk from the beach – the perfect environment to unwind in. Full board is highly recommended; the Turkish cuisine here is first-rate. ⚲ Ulupınar Köyü, Çıralı • Map H5 • (0242) 825 70 96 • www.kibalahotel.com • €€€

5 Tekkebaşi Dervish Lodge, Fethiye

Perched high in the mountains between Kalkan and Fethiye, this unusual lodge offers a genuine alternative to beach tourism. (The nearest beach is an hour's walk downhill; the return journey takes two.) Guests are accommodated in stone huts, nomadic-style tents or hammocks. ⚲ Karağaç Köyü Alınca Mah, Tekkebaşi Mevkii Eşen • Map E5 • (0252) 679 11 42 • www.dervishlodge.com • €€

6 Yonca Resort, Göcek

This family-run hotel has eight tastefully furnished rooms overlooking a courtyard and pool. Visitors often remark that staying here is like being a guest in a family home. ⚲ Cumhuriyet Mah • Map D5 • (0252) 645 22 55 • www.yoncaresort.com • €€€

7 Nesrin's Bademli Ev, Kale

At this simple but characterful hotel in a tiny village near Üğaçiz, guests enjoy home cooking on a lovely terrace shaded by palm trees and bougainvillea. ⚲ Üçagiz Kale Köyü, Demre • Map G6 • (0242) 874 21 70 • www.askamarine.com/bademliev.htm • €€€€

8 Owlsland, Kalkan

Hard to find but well worth the effort, Owlsland occupies a restored 19th-century farm building near the village of Bezirgan, 15 minutes' drive from the coast. The perfect spot for rural relaxation, it has homely ensuite rooms and serves a mouthwatering choice of local dishes. ⚲ Nr Bezirgan village • Map E6 • (0242) 837 52 14 • www.owlsland.com • €€

9 Eko Motel, Köprülü Canyon

This rural retreat lies a short distance from the Köprüçay River, where rafting tours negotiate Köprülü Canyon's choppy waters. On offer are snug bungalows, rooms in stone houses and space for tents, along with a great choice of food; the fresh trout is fabulous. ⚲ Karabük Köyü Beşkonak, Manavgat • Map J4 • (0242) 765 32 01 • www.kanyonlodge.com • €

10 Villa Lapin, Manavgat

Featuring a quirky blend of Ottoman and rustic styles, Villa Lapin is a cosy hotel with a pretty riverside garden. Guests can sample delicious home-made dishes on a rickety wooden terrace overlooking the river, or join one of the regular boat trips organized by the owners. ⚲ Şelale Mah, K Evler 3 • Map K5 • (0242) 742 91 46 • €€

General Index

Page numbers in **bold** type refer to main entries.

Acknowledgements

The Author
Matt Willis is a widely published travel writer whose numerous journeys throughout Turkey have instilled in him a fascination for the country's culture and history. He is also the author of DK's *Top Ten Moscow*, and co-author of DK's Eyewitness guides to Bulgaria, Eastern Europe and Central Europe.

Produced by
Coppermill Books

Editorial Director
Chris Barstow

Designer
Ian Midson

Factchecker
Batur Kiziltuğ

Proofreader
Scarlett O'Hara

Indexer
Helen Peters

Main Photographer
Nigel Hicks

Additional Photography
Kate Clow, Andy Crawford, Trish Gant, Steve Gorton, John Heseltine, Jamie Marshall, Ian O'Leary, Matt Oldfield, Gary Ombler, Terry Richardson, Clive Streeter, Tony Souter, Dominic Whiting, Francesca Yorke

Maps
Jasneet Arora,
Rajesh Kumar Mishra

Assistant Cartography Manager
Suresh Kumar

FOR DORLING KINDERSLEY
Publisher
Vivien Antwi

Publishing Manager
Christine Stroyan

Project Editors
Rada Radojicic,
Alexandra Whittleton

Senior Editor
Sadie Smith

Designer
Tracy Smith

Design Manager
Mabel Chan

Picture Researcher
Ellen Root

DTP Designer
Jason Little

Cartographic Editor
Stuart James

Production Controller
Louise Daly

Picture Credits

t-top, tl-top left; tlc-top left centre; tc-top centre; tr-top right; cla-centre left above; ca-centre above; cra-centre right above; cl-centre left; c-centre; cr-centre right; clb-centre left below; cb-centre below; crb-centre right below; bl-bottom left, b-bottom; bc-bottom centre; bcl-bottom centre left; br-bottom right; d-detail.

The publishers would like to thank the following individuals, companies and picture libraries for permission to reproduce their photographs:

ALAMY IMAGES: Alan Novelli 28–9c.

CORBIS: The Art Archive/Alfredo Dagli Orti 34bl; Bettmann 35cl; epa/Kerim Okten 38tl; Randy Faris 114–15; Jon Arnold Images/ Gavin Hellier 94–5; Richard T. Nowitz 48tr; Jose Fuste Raga 104–5; Nik Wheeler 17br.

GETTY IMAGES: Flickr/Julian Ward 64c; Panoramic Images 12–13c; Riser/Hugh Sitton 24–5c.

HOTEL BERKERANCH: 65bl.

Courtesy of the NATURAL HISTORY MUSEUM, London: Colin Keates 20cb.

TURKISH CULTURE AND TOURISM OFFICE: 118tl.

All other images are © Dorling Kindersley. For further information see www.dkimages.com

Special Editions of DK Travel Guides

DK Travel Guides can be purchased in bulk quantities at discounted prices for use in promotions or as premiums. We are also able to offer special editions and personalized jackets, corporate imprints, and excerpts from all of our books, tailored specifically to meet your own needs.

To find out more, please contact:
(in the United States) **SpecialSales@dk.com**
(in the UK) **TravelSpecialSales@uk.dk.com**
(in Canada) DK Special Sales at **general@tourmaline.ca**
(in Australia) **business.development@pearson.com.au**

Phrase Book

Pronunciation
Turkish uses a Roman alphabet of 29 letters: 8 vowels and 21 consonants. Letters that differ from the English alphabet are: c, pronounced "j" as in "jolly"; ç, pronounced "ch" as in "church"; ğ, which lengthens the preceding vowel and is not pronounced; ı, pronounced "uh"; ö, pronounced "ur" (as in "further"); ş, pronounced "sh" as in "ship"; and ü, pronounced "ew" as in "few".

In an Emergency
Help!	İmdat!	eem-**dat**
Call a doctor!	Bir doktor çağrın!	beer dok-**tor** **chah**-ruhn
Call an ambulance!	Bir ambulans çağrın!	beer am-boo-**lans** **chah**-ruhn
Call the police!	Polis çağrın!	po-**lees chah**-ruhn
Fire!	Yangın!	yan-**guhn**
Where is the nearest telephone/ hospital?	En yakın telefon/ hastane nerede?	en ya-**kuhn** teh-leh-**fon**/ has-ta-**neh** **neh**-reh-deh

Communication Essentials
Yes	Evet	eh-**vet**
No	Hayır	h-'**eye**'-uhr
Thank you	Teşekkür ederim	teh-shek-**kewr eh**-deh-reem
Please	Lütfen	**lewt**-fen
Excuse me	Affedersiniz	**af**-feh-der-see-neez
Hello	Merhaba	**mer**-ha-ba
Goodbye	Hoşça kalın	hosh-**cha ka**-luhn
Morning	Sabah	sa-**bah**
Afternoon	Öğleden sonra	ur-leh-**den son**-ra
Evening	Akşam	ak-**sham**
Yesterday	Dün	dewn
Today	Bugün	**boo**-gewn
Tomorrow	Yarın	**ya**-ruhn
Here	Burada	**boo**-ra-da
There	Şurada	**shoo**-ra-da
What?	Ne?	neh
When?	Ne zaman?	**neh za**-man
Where?	Nerede	**neh**-reh-deh

Useful Phrases
Pleased to meet you	Memnun oldum	mem-**noon ol**-doom
Where is/are?	nerede?	**neh**-reh-deh
How far is it to?	ne kadar uzakta?	neh **ka**-dar oo-zak-ta
Do you speak English?	İngilizce biliyor musunuz?	een-gee-**leez**-jeh bee-**lee**-yor moo-soo-nooz?
I don't understand	Anlamıyorum	an-**la**-muh-yo-room
Can you help me?	Bana yardım edebilir misiniz?	ba-**na** yar-**duhm** eh-deh-bee-**leer** mee-see-neez?
I don't want	istemiyorum	ees-**teh**-mee-yo-room

Useful Words
big	büyük	bew-**yewk**
small	küçük	kew-**chewk**
hot	sıcak	suh-**jak**
cold	soğuk	soh-**ook**
good/well	iyi	ee-**yee**
bad	kötü	kur-**tew**
open	açık	a-**chuhk**
closed	kapalı	ka-pa-**luh**
left	sol	sol
right	sağ	saa
near	yakın	ya-**kuhn**
far	uzak	oo-**zak**
up	yukarı	yoo-ka-**ruh**

down	aşağı	a-shah-**uh**
early	erken	er-**ken**
late	geç	gech
toilets	tuvaletler	too-va-let-**ler**

Shopping
How much is this?	Bu kaç lira?	boo **kach** lee-ra
I would like	istiyorum	ees-**tee**-yo-room
Do you have?	var mı?	**var** muh?
Do you take credit cards?	Kredi kartı kabul ediyor musunuz?	**kreh**-dee **kar**-tuh ka-**bool** eh-**dee**-yor moo-soo-nooz?
What time do you open/ close?	Saat kaçta açılıyor/ kapanıyor?	Sa-**at** kach-**ta** a-chuh-**luh**-yor/ ka-pa-**nuh**-yor
this one	bunu	boo-**noo**
that one	şunu	shoo-**noo**
expensive	pahalı	pa-ha-**luh**
cheap	ucuz	oo-**jooz**
size (clothes)	beden	beh-**den**
size (shoes)	numara	noo-ma-**ra**
white	beyaz	bay-**yaz**
black	siyah	see-**yah**
red	kırmızı	kuhr-muh-**zuh**
yellow	sarı	sa-**ruh**
green	yeşil	yeh-**sheel**
blue	mavi	ma-**vee**
brown	kahverengi	kah-**veh**-ren-gee
shop	dükkan	dewk-**kan**
That's my last offer	Daha fazla veremem	da-**ha faz**-la veh-**reh**-mem

Types of Shop
antiques shop	antikacı	an-**tee**-ka-juh
bakery	fırın	fuh-**ruhn**
bank	banka	**ban**-ka
book shop	kitapçı	kee-tap-**chuh**
cake shop	pastane	pas-ta-**neh**
chemist's/ pharmacy	eczane	ej-za-**neh**
greengrocer's	manav	ma-**nav**
leather shop	derici	deh-ree-**jee**
market/bazaar	çarşı/pazar	char-**shuh**/pa-**zar**
newsstand	gazeteci	ga-**zeh**-teh-jee
post office	postane	pos-ta-**neh**
shoe shop	ayakkabıcı	'eye'-**yak**-ka-buh-juh
supermarket	süpermarket	sew-per-mar-**ket**
tailor	terzi	ter-**zee**
travel agency	seyahat acentesi	say-ya-**hat** a-jen-teh-**see**

Sightseeing
castle	hisar	hee-**sar**
church	kilise	kee-**lee**-seh
mosque	cami	**ja**-mee
museum	müze	**mew**-zeh
palace	saray	sar-'**eye**'
park	park	park
square	meydan	may-**dan**
information office	danışma bürosu	da-nuhsh-**mah bew**-ro-soo
Turkish bath	hamam	ha-**mam**

Transport
airport	havalimanı	ha-**va**-lee-ma-nuh
bus/coach	otobüs	o-to-**bewss**
bus stop	otobüs durağı	o-to-**bewss** doo-**ra**-uh
coach station	otogar	o-to-**gar**
dolmuş	dolmuş	dol-**moosh**
fare	ücret	ewj-**ret**
ferry	vapur	va-**poor**

sea bus	**deniz**	dch-**neez**
	otobüsü	o-to-**bew**-sew
station	**istasyon**	ees-tas-**yon**
taxi	**taksi**	tak-see
ticket	**bilet**	bee-**let**
ticket office	**bilet**	bee-**let**
	gişesi	gee-sheh-**see**
timetable	**tarife**	ta-ree-**feh**

Staying in a Hotel

Do you have a	**Boş odanız**	bosh o-da-**nuhz**
vacant room?	**var mı?**	var muh?
double room	**iki**	ee-**kee**
	kişilik	kee-shee-**leek**
	bir oda	beer o-**da**
twin room	**çift yataklı**	cheeft ya-**tak**-luh
	bir oda	beer o-**da**
for one person	**tek kişilik**	tek kee-shee-**leek**
room with	**banyolu**	**ban**-yo-loo
a bath	**bir oda**	beer o-**da**
shower	**duş**	doosh
porter	**komi**	ko-**mee**
key	**anahtar**	a-nah-**tar**
room service	**oda servisi**	o-**da** ser-vee-**see**
I have a	**Rezervasyonum**	reh-zer-vas-
reservation	**var**	yo-**noom** var

Eating Out

I want to	**Bir masa**	beer **ma**-sa
reserve	**ayırtmak**	'eye'-uhrt-**mak**
a table	**istiyorum**	ees-**tee**-yo-room
The bill please	**Hesap lütfen**	heh-**sap** lewt-fen
I am a	**Et yemiyorum**	et **yeh**-mee-yo-
vegetarian		room
restaurant	**lokanta**	lo-**kan**-ta
waiter	**garson**	gar-**son**
menu	**yemek**	ye-**mek**
	listesi	lees-teh-see
wine list	**şarap**	sha-**rap**
	listesi	lees-teh-see
breakfast	**kahvaltı**	kah-val-**tuh**
lunch	**öğle**	ur-**leh**
	yemeği	yeh-meh-**ee**
dinner	**akşam yemeği**	ak-**sham**
		yeh-meh-**ee**
starter	**meze**	meh-zeh
main course	**ana yemek**	a-**na** yeh-**mek**
dessert	**tatlı**	tat-**luh**
rare	**az pişmiş**	**az** peesh-meesh
well done	**iyi**	ee-**yee**
	pişmiş	peesh-meesh
glass	**bardak**	bar-**dak**
bottle	**şişe**	shee-**sheh**
knife	**bıçak**	buh-**chak**
fork	**çatal**	cha-**tal**
spoon	**kaşık**	ka-**shuhk**

Menu Decoder

balık	ba-**luhk**	fish
bira	**bee**-ra	beer
bonfile	**bon**-fee-leh	fillet steak
buz	booz	ice
çay	ch-'eye'	tea
çorba	chor-**ba**	soup
dana eti	da-**na** eh-**tee**	veal
dondurma	don-door-**ma**	ice cream
ekmek	ek-**mek**	bread
et	et	meat
fırında	fuh-ruhn-**da**	roast
fıstık	fuhs-**tuhk**	pistachio nuts
gazoz	ga-**zoz**	fizzy drink
hurma	hoor-ma	dates
içki	eech-**kee**	alcohol
incir	een-**jeer**	figs
ızgara	uhz-**ga**-ra	charcoal grilled
kahve	kah-**veh**	coffee
kara biber	ka-**ra** bee-**ber**	black pepper
karışık	ka-ruh-**shuhk**	mixed

kaymak	k-'eye'-**mak**	cream
kıyma	kuhy-**ma**	minced meat
köfte	kurf-**teh**	meatballs
kuzu eti	koo-**zoo** eh-tee	lamb
lokum	lo-**koom**	Turkish delight
maden suyu	ma-**den** soo-**yoo**	mineral water
		(fizzy)
meyve suyu	may-**veh** soo-**yoo**	fruit juice
midye	**meed**-yeh	mussels
patlıcan	pat-luh-**jan**	aubergine
peynir	pay-**neer**	cheese
pilav	pee-**lav**	rice
piliç	pee-**leech**	roast chicken
şarap	sha-**rap**	wine
şeker	sheh-**ker**	sugar
su	soo	water
süt	sewt	milk
tavuk	ta-**vook**	chicken
tereyağı	teh-**reh**-yah-uh	butter
tuz	tooz	salt
yoğurt	yoh-**urt**	yoghurt
yumurta	yoo-moor-**ta**	egg
zeytinyağı	zay-**teen**-yah-uh	olive oil

Numbers

0	**sıfır**	**suh**-fuhr
1	**bir**	beer
2	**iki**	ee-**kee**
3	**üç**	ewch
4	**dört**	durt
5	**beş**	besh
6	**altı**	al-**tuh**
7	**yedi**	yeh-**dee**
8	**sekiz**	seh-**keez**
9	**dokuz**	doh-**kooz**
10	**on**	on
11	**on bir**	**on** beer
12	**on iki**	**on** ee-kee
13	**on üç**	**on** ewch
14	**on dört**	**on** durt
15	**on beş**	**on** besh
16	**on altı**	**on** al-tuh
17	**on yedi**	**on** yeh-dee
18	**on sekiz**	**on** seh-keez
19	**on dokuz**	**on** doh-kooz
20	**yirmi**	yeer-**mee**
21	**yirmi bir**	yeer-mee **beer**
30	**otuz**	o-**tooz**
40	**kırk**	kuhrk
50	**elli**	eh-**lee**
60	**altmış**	alt-**muhsh**
70	**yetmiş**	yet-**meesh**
80	**seksen**	sek-**sen**
90	**doksan**	dok-**san**
100	**yüz**	yewz
200	**iki yüz**	ee-**kee** yewz
1,000	**bin**	been
100,000	**yüz bin**	**yewz** been
1,000,000	**bir milyon**	**beer** meel-**yon**

Time

one minute	**bir dakika**	**beer** da-**kee**-ka
one hour	**bir saat**	**beer** sa-at
half an hour	**yarım saat**	ya-**ruhm** sa-at
day	**gün**	gewn
week	**hafta**	haf-**ta**
month	**ay**	'eye'
year	**yıl**	yuhl
Sunday	**pazar**	pa-**zar**
Monday	**pazartesi**	pa-**zar**-teh-see
Tuesday	**salı**	sa-**luh**
Wednesday	**çarşamba**	char-sham-**ba**
Thursday	**perşembe**	per-shem-**beh**
Friday	**cuma**	joo-**ma**
Saturday	**cumartesi**	joo-**mar**-teh-see

Selected Index of Places

Turkey's Southwest Coast: Selected Index of Places